party ! food

party! food

Lorna Wing

Photography by Jan Baldwin

conran
OCTOPUS

First published in 1998 by
Conran Octopus Limited
37 Shelton Street
London WC2H 9HN

A catalogue record of this book is available
from the British Library.
ISBN 1-84091-020-8

Commissioning Editor: Suzannah Gough
Consultant Cookery Editor: Jenni Muir
Proofreader/Indexer: Keith Davidson
Americanization: Norma MacMillan

Art Director: Leslie Harrington
Art Editor: Mary Staples
Photographer: Jan Baldwin
Home Economist: Lindsey Greensted-Benech
Stylist: Sue Parker
Production: Suzanne Sharpless

Printed in China

contents

Lorna understands how to make a party memorable, for all the right reasons. She combines meticulous planning and stalwart reliability with tasty food and a creative eye.

I first met Lorna in the early eighties, when she was doing the food for the party after one of my son Jasper's fashion shows. One of the things that caught everyone's fancy was the mini-portions of fish and chips served in cones made from the *Financial Times* newspaper, a nice, quirky juxtaposition that has since been imitated by many people. But Lorna got there first.

The other thing that impressed me about Lorna was her quiet efficiency. Not surprisingly, she very quickly acquired an excellent reputation and an enviable list of clients. When, in 1986, we bought the Heal's furniture store on London's Tottenham Court Road, we completely overhauled the shop and introduced a scheme that incorporated a new restaurant. Although she took some convincing, Lorna finally accepted the job of running the restaurant and, for the next five years or so, made a great job of it at the same time as building her catering business.

She succeeded at both because she knows there is nothing worse than bland, soggy, unimaginative food that ends up being hidden in the pots and killing the plants.

Lorna's recipes are colourful, innovative and inspiring, but above all, delicious. How could your guests fail to be impressed by dishes like Brioche filled with Scrambled Eggs & Caviar, or Raspberry & Lemon Syllabub Trifle?

As a lover of good wines, I get irritated when completely inappropriate wines are served, and even then, incorrectly. Lorna knows precisely what wine to have for the occasion and how much will be needed. (What a disaster if you run out halfway through the party.) She can put together a fantastic selection of cocktails and never fails to astound me with such innovative drinks as Oyster Shooters or Chocolate Martinis. Seductive as they are, it's probably not a good idea to try them all in the same evening.

As much as I enjoy cooking for my family and friends, I hate having to work to a time limit. Lorna has the priceless ability to take the stress out of the organization of a party. Seemingly nothing goes wrong at her events and everything runs to plan. She always gives the impression that she is having as much fun as everyone else.

What greater praise can there be?

Terence Conran

fabulous food.... deliciou

fabulous foo

Holding parties is a wonderful excuse to gather

together family and friends in a relaxed environment,

to ply them with interesting food and wine, to have

stimulating conversation and, above all, to have a

great time. In the past twenty years I've probably organized five thousand or

so parties: small ones, large ones, glamorous ones and cosy ones, for the

rich and famous, and for those who are neither. Some have tiny budgets,

whilst others spare no expense. But they all have to work – you don't get a

second chance on someone's special day. Of course I've had my disasters

and learnt from them. There was the occasion when I inadvertently set off

the fire alarm whilst glazing a sugary pudding and eighteen burly firemen

turned up unannounced to join in the party. And then there was the time

when all the power failed during a dinner for five hundred. After such

episodes, I quickly learnt that the most important thing to do was to plan,

double check, check some more and to take nothing for granted. This book

combines the experience of many years spent earning my living from the

party business. It has all you need to know about holding a successful party

and how to prepare the food and drinks that will make it memorable. **Enjoy**

The more planning you can do for a party (apart from impromptu occasions) the better you will enjoy it. Who wants to be slaving away over a hot stove when everyone else is having fun? That is not the point of a party. It is for all concerned to have a good time, and that includes the cook. This section shows how, with a little forethought and list making, you can ensure your party runs smoothly – and that the result is the kind of event you really want to hold. First of all, ask yourself the five essential questions: why, when, where, who and what.

planning

The answers will help you decide the type of party you want to hold. Each decision will have an impact on another. For example, the space you have available will affect the number of people you can invite. You may decide that it is impossible to fit in the numbers you had hoped for but that you are not prepared to ask fewer people. So, an alternative location might need to be found. This could mean hiring a venue requiring you to use one of their approved caterers, which in turn would bring its own set of restrictions. Ultimately, all these decisions will help you to determine another crucial factor: your budget.

Budgeting

Different parties need different budgets, so think carefully about the type of party you want to hold as they have differing cost implications. The many variables will have an impact on how you end up spending your money.

Generally, the least expensive way to entertain is to have a drinks party; at the other end of the scale, a seated meal for lots of people can be extremely costly if it means you will have to hire equipment,

pay professional staff to help you and so on. If you do have to hire equipment from specialist companies, a substantial amount of your budget can be easily swallowed up – if you are able to borrow from family and friends, so much the better. Glasses and bar equipment for drinks parties are usually quite reasonable to hire, whereas hiring tables, chairs, linen, tableware and mobile kitchen equipment can take up a hefty chunk of your expenditure.

When planning a small drinks party or a meal at home where you are serving wines and soft drinks, you will need to spend about equal amounts of money on food and drinks. However, if you are going to serve particularly expensive champagne, wines or foods, that ratio will obviously alter. If you need to keep your costs down, it is best not to offer too much choice of food or drinks.

You need to establish your own priorities and decide where you wish to allocate your budget. For some people, the food served is far more important than the drinks, and for others, the entertainment will take greater priority. Each to his own.

Menu

Only once you know how many people you can invite, can you start planning your menu. Think about the kind of people you are inviting to your party, and why. Are they young or old? Do they tend to have hearty appetites or tiny ones because every calorie is being counted? Are there any specific dietary, religious or medical needs the menu must account for? Or are your guests just plain fussy?

The recipes in this book are arranged into three main sections. Food you can eat in the hand, food you need to eat with a fork, and drinks, alcoholic and non-alcoholic. Choose what suits your personal lifestyle the best. There will be occasions when you want to pull out all of the stops and others when you cannot summon up the energy to cook a single thing – that is fine. I am including recipes that can be done well ahead of time and require little or no cooking, as well as recipes that are a bit more complicated. There are dishes for the new and inexperienced cook and for those who know their way around the kitchen. Most recipes are for ten, but you can easily divide or multiply them to suit your needs.

However it is important to remember that, in the end, it is only food and there is always a solution if disaster strikes. It might be calling the local fish and chip shop and arranging to collect fifty portions of their best. Serve them, still wrapped in newspaper, with that vintage champagne you had been planning to drink. Or boil up all the pasta you can lay your hands on and serve it with four store-cupboard sauces. Your guests are there to enjoy themselves in your company; watching you panic about a culinary disaster will only make them uncomfortable.

signal. It then leaves the rest of the day to kick off your shoes, catch up on the papers and finish off the rest of the bubbly. Breakfasts and brunches worth getting up for are anything with smoked salmon, waffles and bagels, and eggs every possible way. And, of course, copious and reviving quantities of coffee.

For those who want an effortless AM start, this book has ideas for no-cook, buy-absolutely-everything menus to make brunches as painless as possible. And for those who find cooking pleasurable, I am giving lots of hearty one-pot dishes, like my Butter Chicken Masala. A glass of steaming hot frothy chocolate with churros to dip makes a decadent finish to any brunch. Roll on next Sunday!

Lunch & suppers

Lunch can be pizza. Lunch can be pasta. In fact, lunch can be anything you want it to be. Most of all, it should be spontaneous and uncomplicated. Ditto supper. Make it effortless, with as much as possible of the preparation and cooking done way ahead of time.

For these rather informal occasions, try a mixture of finger and fork foods. In warm weather, nibble on some vegetable-based canapés for an appetizer or first course. Follow with an all-in-one salad.

In cold months, make a big cauldron of jambalaya or cheesy polenta, the kind of hearty, sustaining dishes that are enough to rid anyone of the winter blues. Do not ignore sandwiches when you are entertaining informally – they do not have to be the curled-up cheese and tomato

The event

So, what type of event is it to be? Are you celebrating a special, once-in-a-lifetime family occasion such as a wedding or christening? Perhaps Sunday morning is the only time you can spare to have people over. Or, there could be no particular reason to celebrate and you simply want to get together with some fun friends, enjoy a few cocktails and nibble on some snacks.

Fortunately, the rules have now changed about how we entertain at home. Gone are the days of the stuffy three-course meal, invariably eaten in the dining room on the 'best' china.

Nowadays, we are just as likely to be perched on a stool in the kitchen, quaffing wine and giving the cook a hand in-between courses. It is your party, so do what suits you and your lifestyle.

Breakfasts & brunches

Weekends are for brunch and for friends meandering over, newspapers in hand, as and when it suits them. It is flexitime, anywhere between late morning and early afternoon, but never before midday if you have any sense. For me, brunches are the best. It is a time when you can ask friends over knowing that they will not stay as long as an invitation to lunch would

Picnic food must be portable and sturdy enough to withstand the journey. Hand-held food is the most convenient. A collection of savoury pastries is good to snack on during a day at the beach or in the country and can be easily transported in a box.

variety. What about a sizzlingly hot, soft-shelled crab sandwich? Or, the ultimate in chic, a caviar sandwich? At the other end of the scale, you could try a Sloppy Joe of hot and spicy chilli piled into pitta bread, great for those times when you have friends over to down a few beers and to watch the big match on television. Side orders, such as my hot Garlic Potato Crisps and Sweet Potato Fries, make sandwiches into more of an occasion yet are popular with most people.

Picnics & barbecues

Picnics, even if they are only at the end of the garden, must be portable. You have to be able to carry them without the assistance of a Sherpa. So, do not be tempted to take along breakable and weighty tableware – leave it all at home for other, more appropriate, occasions. If you are embarking on a journey, the food has to be well chosen to survive the sweltering heat of a car boot or being carried on your back in a rucksack.

Picnics can run the entire gamut from grandiose and grown-up occasions, to straightforward and simple. But if you are wise, you will decide on the latter. Good eat-in-the-hand foods are often pastry based, such as a goat cheese and courgette [zucchini] pastry, or wrapped items, like my Lettuce-Wrapped Moroccan Meatballs. The same can be said for chunky sandwiches – great for picnics.

Do not forget about winter picnics either; they have their own appeal. Wrap yourself up warmly against the elements and serve something sustaining and hot, like a fruity lamb tagine or red duck curry from a wide-necked thermos flask.

Barbecues are the delight of many a cook. They are a great excuse to be freed from the confines of the indoor kitchen and to relinquish the culinary duties to someone else. Keep barbecues dead simple. Do not be tempted, for one single moment, to make them sophisticated.

Outdoor entertaining makes for heartier appetites and requires robust foods, so supplement the sausages and burgers with sticky Thai chicken wings and marinated vegetable skewers. Throw fat, juicy prawns, still in their shells, onto the barbie, along with a rack or two of ribs. Have ice-cold white wine and lots of non-alcoholic concoctions to hand.

And to finish? Try sweet bruschetta topped with the best of the summer's fruits. Peaches, strawberries, raspberries and a dollop of buttery-yellow clotted cream are a divine combination. Cakes and pastries, bite-sized or a generous wedge, always go down a treat. If all that seems like too much effort, the lazy cook can always substitute rounds of oozing cheeses and baskets of plump fruits, ripe to the point of bursting.

Afternoon tea

Afternoon tea, traditionally taken at four on the dot, is for most of us a relic of the past, so when the opportunity does arise, do it in style! Teatime is an ideal way to enjoy a lazy afternoon with friends and a perfect excuse to indulge in luscious cakes that you would not normally dream of eating. It is also the perfect way to celebrate a christening or wedding.

At such times, the first thing that people want when they arrive is a drink. It could be something innocuous like my glorious frappé of strawberries and cream, or a glass of Long Island Iced Tea (an innocent name for a lethal cocktail).

After the initial drinks have done the rounds, follow up quickly with the food as you will find that everyone is ravenous by this time. Never be amazed at people's capacity to eat on these occasions and always allow more food than you could ever have imagined possible.

Food for tea should be small, or at the most should be capable of being eaten with one hand. Plates are perfectly acceptable for gathering up a little selection of goodies, but forget using forks, except for those sticky cakes.

Cocktail parties

Cocktail parties come in different guises. There are those where guests arrive promptly at the allotted cocktail hour for a glass of champagne and a few exquisite but insubstantial canapés before going on to dinner, or home for supper. And then there are those where you know that guests will not be leaving until the wee small hours of the morning. The former is an excellent way of entertaining lots of people in one fell swoop as it is unlikely that they will all arrive at once. Some

they have a supply of cocktail napkins at the ready for greasy fingers. Pace the food, starting with cold items then moving on to hot. Limit yourself to only one or two that require last-minute attention.

In an ideal world you would probably have one completely effortless canapé, one canapé with a dip, and a bowl of something like the Garlic Potato Crisps that people can happily pick at. Then you might have a crisp vegetable canapé, followed by two bread-based items for a bit of substance. A pastry tart, followed by something deep-fried and very moreish, such as the miniature fish and chips, would round it off nicely. Avoid mixing different canapés on a serving plate as you will create more impact with twenty identical items. It also makes replenishing the dish much faster.

When your cocktail party is going to last for as long as people are having fun, and the food therefore needs to be quite substantial, treat it like a meal and serve it in courses. Start with some small canapés and follow with more filling finger foods, like bruschetta, sandwiches or pizza. Put out small plates for these. Finally, serve some sweet foods, reverting back to bite-sized items again, such as little summer fruit tartlets.

There is another sort of cocktail occasion that is neither canapés nor substantial finger foods. It is simply friends over for snacks and nibbles, maybe stopping off on their way home from work, or coming over on a Saturday night for a housewarming. You do not always want to start from scratch, so this

guests will stay for half an hour, whilst others are there for the duration. At these sorts of cocktail parties the food is bite-sized and generally served. For the latter type of party though, you need to treat it as a mini-buffet, giving guests the qualities of a cocktail party combined with the sustenance of a meal.

The great thing about cocktail parties is that the guests can be a mix of

professional and personal acquaintances. Best of all, it allows everyone to circulate freely, moving on quickly if they get stuck with someone they find boring.

For a two-hour cocktail event, you want only bite-sized canapés so that guests don't have to worry about catching crumbs in one hand whilst balancing a drink in the other. Enlist willing volunteers to help hand out the food, making sure

is when you want to make clever use of
storecupboard ingredients or foods that .
can be whipped out of the freezer.

It might be some Sesame Cheese
Straws and Anchovy Pastries, which will
only take a few minutes to heat up in the
oven. Or, it might be a packet of crisps
[potato chips] over which you toss some
hot garlic butter before warming through.
Herby nuts, spicy olives and jars of
sun-dried tomatoes and marinated
artichokes all belong here with slices of
cheese and salami. Gather this collection
of foods, put them into bowls and arrange
half a dozen on a tray for a stylish way of
making simple foods look good.

As far as drinks are concerned, the
sky's the limit. Good champagne or
sparkling wines are never spurned, nor
are still wines or great, make-ahead,
cocktails. But whatever you decide to
serve, make sure that you always have
mineral water and soft drinks available.
It is often difficult to keep track of how
much you have drunk at parties if your
glass is continually being topped up and
the last thing you want to do if friends are
driving is to send them on their way
having drunk too much alcohol.

What I particularly love about cocktail
parties is that they are a wonderful
opportunity to show off your style. There
are myriad serving dishes you can choose
from to make your mark. Contemporary
steel, glass and perspex give canapés a
modern, sleek look, whilst wooden plates
and baskets lined with grapevine or
banana leaves give a natural, earthy feel.
Take your pick to match your mood.

*Cocktail parties are the best means of entertaining a
large number of people and an ideal way to socialize
with personal and professional acquaintances. Guests
can circulate freely and no one is expected to spend
the entire night talking to one person.*

Bring your own

Bring Your Own or BYO parties, where everyone brings a bottle to drink, can help keep the costs of throwing a party to a minimum. However, if this is your plan, make sure you allow sufficient drinks of your own for everyone to have at least a glass each before relying on any donated bottles. Do not forget that you will need to chill white wines and beers, so either make room in the fridge or order in some extra ice and make sure that you get them chilled as soon as possible as it will take about an hour to get everything to the right temperature.

Another cost-effective way of entertaining is to ask everyone to bring a dish instead of a bottle. But if you plan to do this, remember you still need to organize the menu and be specific about

what you want friends to contribute as you do not want them all turning up with the same food. This type of party is also a good way of spreading the workload if you know you are going to be frantically busy – and it is much more fun than slaving away in the kitchen on your own.

The location

The space you choose for entertaining depends entirely on the kind of party you are giving, as well as the numbers, the weather and your budget. So, deciding on the location, at home or elsewhere, indoors or outdoors, is one of the initial hurdles to overcome.

If the party is to be at home, especially if it is for larger numbers, be inventive. Be prepared to clear out furniture. The hallway could become a dining room. A bedroom could become the bar.

When the space inside your home is not suitable for one reason or another, a tent may be the answer. You might just need to extend your house with a canopy tacked on to the patio, or you may require a large free-standing tent to accommodate the whole party. Be guided by the experts on the type and size of structure. Safety is paramount when erecting temporary structures on slopes or different levels and so there needs to be a balance between aesthetics and practicalities.

Tents, these days, are sophisticated and can be beautifully lined in all shades. It might be the simplicity of pure white pleating. Or it might be the effect of a night sky created by lining the marquee entirely in black and lighting it with

Even at parties where guests are asked to bring their own drinks, make sure you are able to offer at least one glass of alcohol per person before relying on any donated bottles.

hundreds of tiny twinkling lights. Do not forget that in cold months you will also need to organize some form of heating.

For large events at home, expect to have your life disrupted for anything up to a week, particularly if tents are being erected and generators need to be brought in. There will also be numerous deliveries from dawn to dusk. Remember, too, that the party is not over when your guests go home. Some contractors will take everything away with them on the day, but others will need to return to dismantle tents, remove bulky equipment and so on.

If you do decide to hold your party at home, make a realistic appraisal of all the resources you have available. Do not be too ambitious and do not overload your resources. Consider not only your kitchen space, but also your oven, fridge and freezer capacities. Is there enough room in your kitchen to prepare a hot fork lunch for fifty? Do you have sufficient glasses, china, cutlery and all the necessary kitchen paraphernalia for that lunch? If not, do you want, or can you afford, to hire it? Or would it make more sense instead to serve a cold finger food menu, not requiring plates or cutlery? How much time are you likely to have to prepare the food yourself in the run-up to the party and on the day itself? Or will you need some help with the cooking and serving? All these decisions will have an impact on the food and drink that you serve.

It is quite possible that you will have to supplement the furniture and equipment you have at home. There are numerous companies that hire out tables, chairs, china, glassware, tablecloths and mobile kitchens, including ovens, fridges and freezers, from the very mundane to the extremely elaborate. If it does not cost you

Party checklist

I find the best way to approach organizing a party, large or small, is to 'walk the course' in my head from start to finish. Think about where guests will park their cars; where a cloakroom needs to be set up for coats; if a receiving line, informal or otherwise, is required and where the first drinks will be served from. Where should the tables and chairs be situated?

Are you going to dance and, if so, is there a suitable dance floor, or will you need to bring one in? What decorations, floral or otherwise, are needed for the tables and room? Consider the best place acoustically for musicians to set up. Is the lighting adequate, or does it need to be supplemented with candles and specialist lighting? Importantly, do you have sufficient power for all of this lighting, cooking and entertainment? Only then can you start to plan your party properly.

This checklist is a quick reminder of everything you need to remember when organizing a party. Some points only apply to small parties whilst others are particular to large parties, however you will find every event runs more smoothly when you adhere to this basic timetable.

In advance

● Decide what type of party you want to hold, whether it is seated or standing, formal or informal, large or small
● Determine your budget
● Compile your guest list
● Set the date
● Calculate if you have sufficient space and kitchen facilities (ovens, fridges, freezers etc) to hold your party at home, or if you need to hire a venue. If hiring, choose and book the venue
● Contact and get quotes from suppliers, including caterers, tents, florists, mobile toilets, musicians, dance floors, lighting, power supplies, mobile air conditioning or heaters Have a look at examples of their work
● Check you have enough tableware, serving dishes, linen, kitchen equipment, etc. If not, find out if there is anyone you can borrow from, or get a quote for hiring equipment

● Send out invitations, or invite guests by telephone, but only once you know you can do what you want, where you want and within your budget. Keep a record of acceptances and any special dietary needs
● Choose the menu, using a varied mix of ingredients, textures, colours, balance of flavours and seasonal foods. Try to choose several dishes that can be prepared well in advance of the party and remember any guests with special dietary needs
● Choose the drinks
● Make detailed shopping lists and order food, the celebratory cake, drinks, ice, equipment, music, flowers, decorations etc, as appropriate. Buy any unperishable items
● Cook and freeze any dishes that can be prepared in advance
● Write or get menus and placecards printed
● Book staff, if needed. Check if they or any other contractors need a meal
● Warn the neighbours

Just before or on the day

● Shop for the remaining food and drinks, plus flowers and any other decorations
● Prepare the food
● Check that everything you have ordered has been delivered
● Arrange flowers and any decorations
● Put out all glasses, plates, linen, serving dishes etc
● Chill the drinks and make any cocktails that can be prepared in advance
● Organize a space for guests to leave coats
● Organize a space to put any dirty plates and glasses
● Have clean bins ready to take any rubbish
● Place clean hand towels and soaps in the bathrooms
● Brief staff or any people helping with the food or drink

● **Party!**

any extra, get the equipment in the day before so that you have time to unpack and check it all. Most firms will charge you to take everything back dirty but it is worth paying extra for this service as it will save you hours of washing up.

If you decide that the party cannot be at home, one of your first challenges is finding a suitable venue as so many get booked months in advance. There are many different types of venues available, from museums to village halls, to club houses and historic houses. Look for them in the Yellow Pages, call the National Trust, peruse your local papers or consult dedicated venue guides.

Your decision about where to go will depend on availability, numbers and decor. Many venues have restrictions about what you can and cannot do. Some will accommodate your every need, allowing you to take in your favourite caterer and florist and will let you drink, smoke and dance to your heart's content. Then there are other venues where there will be restrictions that will determine whether you want to hold your party there after all. Many museums and historic houses have very specific rules about their buildings and how they are used by outsiders. Sometimes you will have to choose the caterer, lighting people, florist and entertainers from an approved list.

The behind-the-scenes area is as important as what goes on front-of-house, as it will have a major effect on much of your decision making. If your home, or the hired venue, does not have sufficient kitchen space, is there another suitable area to build a temporary mobile kitchen? I have set up kitchens in barns with resident bats, in basements when dinner was being served three floors up, and in

buildings that were still incomplete and exposed to all the elements. Caterers are used to being very enterprising when it comes to finding space for their kitchens!

Remember to locate an area to leave all the dirty plates, cutlery and glasses, as well as empty bottles and rubbish. If the bathroom facilities are poor, pretty them up with your own soaps and hand towels.

The atmosphere

Once you have chosen where the party is going to be, decide if you are going to theme it in any way. It does not have to be overtly themed, or indeed at all, but it does help to give focus to the flowers, table decorations and so on. There is no need to go over the top and make all the food match the colours of the room: food should be for real, not made to fit a theme.

Remember that creating an exciting, interesting mood for a party starts at the front door. First impressions do count and set the tone for what is happening inside. Decorate entrances in a style appropriate to the party, be it with flowers, foilage, banners or fabric. When it is dark, create a magical mood by hanging votive lights in trees, or make a candlelit walkway with a row of garden flares.

Scents too can enhance the mood and hint at what is in store. Use room sprays or scented oils, burn incense, choose beautifully perfumed pot pourris or, for weddings, a romantic flutter of scented fresh petals. In winter, try warm, spicy fragrances such as cinnamon, nutmeg and vanilla; for summertime, you want fresh citrus, floral or herbaceous scents.

Music & dancing

The music at a party should be memorable, but for the right reasons. Not only should it make an impact, it should enhance and complement the whole event. Music can be cleverly used to theme a party and match the atmosphere you want to create. There is such an array of styles to choose from, whether it is a salsa or jive band, a cocktail pianist, 1930s French café swing jazz, a string orchestra or even Elizabethan minstrels.

For parties such as large family gatherings, where people of all different ages are attending, there is no quick-fix formula for choosing the music as taste is such a personal thing. But what you do not want to do is alienate anyone by playing solely one style. If you are organizing the party music yourself, there are some good commercially produced, ready-mixed CDs and party tapes on the market which cover a broad spectrum of tastes. Or you could ask each guest to bring their favourite CD, along with a bottle, for a real variety of music.

When you are employing professional musicians or DJs, make sure that you spend time with them before the party and tell them your likes and dislikes. Be very clear about the sort of mood and atmosphere you want to create as it takes great skill and experience to play the right music at a party and to judge the mood of the group accurately.

Music does not have to be loud or deafening to be good, but it does have to be at the right volume. Try to contain music in one area so that guests can move away from it if they want some peace and quiet for talking. Be considerate about the noise levels if you are in a residential area and do not want to upset your neighbours.

Most musicians will have an opinion about the ideal place to be positioned in a room for the best acoustics, but all will agree that they want to be in the same room as the party. If you put them in a second room they will be too cut off and you will not only lose the atmosphere but split the party completely. Do not forget that musicians need regular breaks from playing, so you might need to think about having an alternative source of music while they are resting.

Remember that sound systems will need extra power points and sufficient power, so make sure that you have enough of both. Ensure that all extension leads or cables are securely taped down

to prevent any accidents and that they are safely positioned so they cannot get wet.

If you are planning a large party where everyone is going to dance, it is always best to lay a parquet or wooden floor as it is very hard to dance on an uneven surface like matting. And if you are going to the expense of paying for a band, it is false economy not to have a dance floor as well. Small dance floors are the most effective as they create an intimacy that a large floor can never achieve. Ideally, this dance floor should be centrally positioned in a room with tables and chairs all around to best enjoy the music and create a party atmosphere.

Lighting

Lighting has a crucial part to play in setting the atmosphere for a party. Candlelight hides a multitude of sins and can make the most dingy of places look stunning. Use masses of candles, of every different shape and size, to transform a space. Make sure that they are positioned in safe places away from anything likely to catch light such as flowers, fabric, or if outside, dry grass. I never leave candles unattended, nor put them at floor level where it is easy for clothing to catch light. Keep a fire extinguisher to hand if you plan to have lots of burning candles.

Storm vases, kerosene lamps and votive candles are all great for outside lighting, grouped together or singly. Try to ring the changes. For example, during the festive season, put nightlights into highly polished red and green apples. Cut a bit from the base so that it sits securely and

A colourful collection of candles makes a pretty table decoration as well as an atmospheric form of lighting. Make sure the flames are kept away from anything that may catch light and never leave them unattended in case of an accident.

then scoop out the centre to take the candle. The same can be done with globe artichokes. To extend the life of the candles, pop them into the freezer for a few hours to slow down their burning.

For large or special parties, lighting experts can create magical effects with up-lighters, down-lighters, shaded table lamps and myriad different lighting techniques. They will outline driveways with flaming torchères, put twinkling lights in trees, bathe rooms with a warm glow, down-light table centrepieces and create drama on dance floors. They will be sensitive to the mood of the party and can even change the lighting during the course of the evening. You may start, for example, with lighting clear enough so that guests can see everything, then move onto subdued, warmer lighting later on.

Flowers & table decorations

When decorating rooms and tables, decide where you want to concentrate your efforts and money. It might be with a single glorious flower arrangement, or tying napkins with frivolous polka-dot or candy-striped ribbons. If flowers are what you want, raid the garden, go to the flower market at the crack of dawn, or involve your favourite florist.

Florists and decorators can bring originality, drama and ingenuity to a party. They will help you select a theme for the occasion, be it modern or period, simple or elaborate, and offer arrangements that are tropical, scented or edible. They will be eminently practical in advising you on colour schemes, settings and which blooms to avoid to stay within budget.

Matching flowers and foliage (and vegetables and fruits) to containers is

essential and should tie in with your personal style, taste and surroundings. Choose from stone, glass, wood, pottery, wicker, china or metal containers.

You do not have to spend a fortune on decorating tables, nor do they always have to be decorated with flowers. I like having edible table arrangements. Little tubs of sprouting mustard and cress, grouped together in a low wooden box, are effective and inexpensive for a spare, minimalist look. Hollowed-out pumpkin and squash, in autumn months, make natural containers for seedheads, berries and teasels from the hedgerow. For an ethnic feel, pile brightly coloured spices like turmeric and paprika into pyramid shapes in shallow metal bowls, Indian-style. Do the same with red and green chillies, rice, lentils or aromatic star anise. Try to develop your own style and do it with a bit of wit and humour. There is nothing to stop you having a goldfish idly swimming around in a clear glass bowl to decorate an Oriental buffet table.

Raid cupboards and drawers and use your imagination to see what you have already got that can be used. Blankets, throws and sheets can double as tablecloths. Do not hesitate to give each table a different look if necessary, if it means not having to buy or hire tablelinens. Or borrow from friends. Remember, everything does not have to match. You may decide on a pale and interesting look, with everything in shades of white and cream. Then again, bright, bold and clashing might be more to your

taste. Equally, it could be your much-used kitchen china and prized but battered family silver, jazzed up with napkins tied with raffia and flowering herbs. Be bold in whatever you do. Cut over-sized leaves from the garden to use as tablemats; use shells for salt and pepper. Line plates or bowls with squares of banana leaves for an inexpensive Asian look.

Hand-write menus and put them into picture frames. Or, for a buffet table, write the name of each dish on a gift tag and tie it to a pear sprayed gold and placed alongside the dish. For an Oriental theme, write your menu and a few Chinese symbols on rice paper, tie with a silky tassel, or secure with bright red sealing

wax. Placecards or menus poked into fortune cookies are fun and original. So are names written in gold or silver pen on large smooth pebbles or glossy green leaves.

Invitations

If you do not want the expense of printing menus and invitations, do your own. Invitations, whether hand-written, faxed or formally engraved, should state clearly who is doing what, where and when. Most importantly, tell your guests what the dress code is. Everyone, regardless how much of a party-goer they are, wants to know what to wear. You should also provide a map or instructions if your home or the location is difficult to find.

Waiting staff: 1 per 20 guests for serving food and drinks. When you have more than 1 waiter, split the duties of serving the food and drink between them.

Bar staff: 1 per 100 guests when only champagne, wine, water and soft drinks are being served. Drinks made to order take much more time to make than just opening a bottle of wine and pouring it. So, if you are serving cocktails, or have a full bar, you will need to have a minimum of 2 per 100 guests.

Cooks: 1 per 50 guests. Whilst a professional chef can usually cope with assembling 400 hot and cold canapés or finger food items over a 2 hour period, you would need 2 experienced cooks to manage the same quantities. This assumes that there are not too many items needing last-minute attention.

FORK FOOD PARTIES

Waiting staff: 1 per 15 guests for serving food and drinks at a stand-up event. When you have more than 1 waiter, split the duties of serving the food and drink between them. For serving food at a seated event, allow 1 waiter per 10, and for serving drinks allow 1 waiter per 20.

Bar staff: see above.

Cooks: 1 per 20 to 25 guests. This depends on the variety of dishes and whether the food is hot or cold. It also assumes that most of the preparation has been done and all that is needed is the final assembling or reheating.

Hiring caterers and party planners

Some large-scale parties need to be treated almost like a military exercise. This is where caterers and party planners really come into their own as they can guide you through the potential entertaining minefields. If you have decided to hand over all the planning to a caterer, first insist on a tasting, unless you are already familiar with their food. It is your party so you want to be assured that your expectations will be met. Taste the menu and the wines to go with it.

In addition, ask to see the table laid if you plan to have a seated meal. Check that you like the style and quality of the chairs, linen and tableware – it is such an individual thing and what suits one person may not suit another. Ask, too, to have a sample flower arrangement for the table to make sure that, apart from liking it, you are also able to see your guests over the top of it.

Unsure of the musicians? Ideally, go and hear them play before you finally make up your mind, or failing that, ask for a tape of their work so that you can listen to the music at home.

If you are the one overseeing the whole thing, make sure that all your outside contractors are working together. For instance, the tent company will have to liaise with the lighting people, caterer, musicians and florist to ensure that they all have enough space to work in and that the tent will be ready in time to allow the others to do their bit.

If your budget does not run to hiring a professional photographer to record all your party efforts, place some disposable cameras on the tables for guests to snap pictures instead.

Helping hands

Try, if you can, to get some help with serving the food. If you cannot afford to hire waiting staff or cooks, or it simply is not that kind of party, ask friends, family or teenage children to lend a hand, but make sure that you give them specific duties. Go through every step of the event. Brief them well before the party on exactly what you expect them to do and show them where everything goes. As timing is so important at parties, you will find it highly advantageous to have a schedule which says who is doing what and at what time.

There may be some occasions, such as large parties or special celebrations, when you will definitely need some professional help. The Yellow Pages or local catering colleges are good places to start looking for staff.

At large parties in particular, you will also need somebody to oversee and manage it all, as well as waiting staff, bar staff, cooks, washer-uppers and a strong body to do all the fetching and carrying. If that is the case, the list on the left is a useful guideline about the numbers of staff you will require. They should arrive about 1½ to 2 hours before the party in order to set up bars, chill wines, lay any tables and finish preparing the food.

Make sure that you designate a private area with a coat rail and hangers for all these people to leave their coats and personal belongings in safety. Determine whose responsibility it is to feed them and also any contractor's crew.

Finally, do not forget that you will probably have to contribute to the cost of their transport home if the party will be finishing late at night.

Cleaning up

The day before a party I always try to get the house sorted so that all I have to think about on the day itself is finishing off the food, opening bottles and getting myself ready. Moving furniture, cleaning, arranging flowers and so forth always takes much longer than you expect, so ideally, if you have the space and your lifestyle allows it, do as much as possible a day in advance.

Make space in the wardrobe so that there is somewhere for guests to hang their coats. Move any unnecessary furniture to allow space for everyone to circulate freely. Sort out hand towels for the bathroom, along with a small sewing kit for repairs and a first aid kit ready for emergencies. So you do not get inundated with requests for the local taxi service, pin up the telephone number by each phone.

Even when the 'staff' are friends and family, make sure you give them specific duties to attend to and brief them on the schedule so that everybody knows who is doing what and when. Ask them to arrive about two hours beforehand to help set up.

Sort out all the serving dishes that you want to use, arrange flowers, set up the bar and put wines in the fridge to chill.

Once all that has been done, make a list of everything there is left to do on the day along with a loose timing schedule next to each task. Finally, fill a bucket with water ready to plunge gifts of flowers into so you do not have to spend time arranging them in the midst of the party.

Cleaning up after a party really brings you down to earth with a bump. If you can, get some help with the washing up during the party so you are not left with all the chaos later on. If you do not have any help and cannot face all that cleaning up immediately, get organized beforehand. Clear a space, preferably out of sight, so that you can stack all the dirty dishes in neat piles as you go, line up glasses and put cutlery into a large bowl of soapy water to soak. Then, throw a cloth over the top and forget about it until later. It is best to dispose of empty bottles in cardboard boxes rather than plastic bags, so keep a few stacked beside the bin ready. Empty ashtrays before going to bed, open windows to freshen up the house and clear the air. Then face it all the next day.

The neighbours

Inform neighbours if you are planning a large party where there will be lots of activity with people parking cars, making noise and coming and going at all hours. Most neighbours are pretty tolerant, unless you are a habitual noisy party giver who keeps them awake until the small hours. Whenever I have a party, I send a note outlining what is happening with the expected finishing time, and deliver it with a small bunch of flowers or a bottle of wine. It always works wonders.

FINGER FOOD PARTIES
- Tables, occasional tables and any extra tables for the bar, food preparation, or for holding dirty glasses, plates etc
- Tablecloths for the tables and bar
- Linen napkins for the bar and waiters
- Linen or paper napkins for guests
- Chairs
- Coat rails and hangers. Provide a ticketing system for large parties
- Dustbins or large plastic tubs for chilling drinks and also for rubbish
- Plastic sheeting for floor of bar area
- Glasses: champagne, wine, tumblers, cocktail, highballs, liqueur or brandy
- Jugs for juice
- Ice bucket and spoon
- Drinks trays
- Corkscrews and bottle openers
- Blender, shaker, strainer, long-handled spoon, drinks measures
- Small board, sharp knife and bowl for fruit for drinks
- Ashtrays
- Dish towels and hand towels
- Serving dishes and bowls
- Kitchen equipment, ovens, hot cupboards, fryers, fridge, freezer, baking trays, saucepans, mixing bowls, etc
- Ice for chilling and putting into drinks
- Disposables, first-aid kit, candles, tapers, matches, cocktail sticks, loo paper, soap, rubbish bags, plastic bags, paper towels, plastic wrap, foil and cleaning cloths

FORK FOOD PARTIES
- All the above equipment
- Tables if seating is required
- Tablecloths if seating is required
- Dinner plates and forks
- Dessert plates and spoons or forks
- Serving spoons and forks
- Sauce spoons
- Salt and pepper mills
- Coffee or tea cups and saucers
- Coffee or tea pots
- Sugar bowls and cream jugs
- Kettles, water or coffee urns

For those people who are undecided about how they want to entertain, I have put together a versatile menu planning chart to help devise menus for parties, be they small and intimate, or large and informal. This at-a-glance guide can help you make up your mind and give you an idea of the type and quantity of food you will need. Use the chart for all types of events: for casual brunches with your nearest and dearest, for that chic cocktail party when you want to impress, or even to advise your caterer if you are not up to organizing a family wedding on your own.

Perhaps it is high summer and you want to ask a dozen friends over. If so, scan the chart. You may decide to invite them for a mixture of finger and fork food, serving some canapés, followed by a cold main, salad and a pudding. Alternatively, you could skip the meal and serve simple finger food instead. If your usual lifestyle

menu planning

	Finger Food Only		Finger and Fork Food		Fork Food Only	
	SUMMER	WINTER	SUMMER	WINTER	SUMMER	WINTER
10-20 PEOPLE	6 cold savouries *8-12 items each*	4 cold savouries 2 hot savouries *8-12 items each*	2 cold canapés *3 items each* 1 cold fork dish 1 salad 1 bread 1 cold dessert	2 cold canapés *3 items each* 1 hot fork dish 1 salad 1 bread 1 cold dessert	1 cold fork dish 1 salad 1 bread 1 cold dessert	1 hot fork dish 1 salad 1 bread 1 cold dessert
30-40 PEOPLE	8 cold savouries *8-12 items each*	5 cold savouries 3 hot savouries *8-12 items each*	3 cold canapés *3 items each* 2 cold fork dishes 2 salads 1 bread 1 cold dessert	2 cold canapés 1 hot canapé *3 items each* 1 cold fork dish 1 hot fork dish 1 cold salad 1 hot vegetable dish 1 bread 1 cold dessert	2 cold fork dishes 1 salad 1 bread 1 cold dessert	1 cold fork dish 1 hot fork dish 1 salad 1 bread 1 cold dessert
50-60 PEOPLE	7 cold savouries 1 cold sweet *8-12 items each*	4 cold savouries 3 hot savouries 1 cold sweet *8-12 items each*	3 cold canapés *3 items each* 2 cold fork dishes 1 hot fork dish 2 salads 1 bread 2 cold desserts	2 cold canapés 1 hot canapé *3 items each* 1 cold fork dish 1 hot fork dish 1 salad 1 hot vegetable dish 1 bread 2 cold desserts	3 cold fork dishes 2 salads 1 bread 2 cold desserts	1 cold fork dish 2 hot fork dishes 1 salad 1 hot vegetable dish 1 bread 1 cold dessert 1 hot dessert

is frenetic, you hurriedly shop for parties on the way home from work and there is never enough time to cook, do not even think about choosing a menu needing lots of last-minute attention. Instead, deliberately plan one that can be prepared a day or two ahead and only needs the minimum of attention before serving.

There are some ground rules about good menu planning. Think about all of the following when using the chart.

● Have a varied mix of ingredients, including fish and meat, dairy products, pasta, rice or grains, and some fruits and vegetables too.

● Try not to repeat ingredients in the same menu, such as serving chicken twice, say, in a canapé topping and again in a salad.

● Have a contrast of textures, soft and crisp, as well as smooth and rough.

● Include a good spectrum of colours in the menu, from pale and interesting foods, to bold and bright.

● You will not want to have the entire range of these flavours in one menu, but think carefully about a balance of sweet versus sour, savoury or bitter, salty or sharp, as well as smoky and flowery.

Entertaining will always be enjoyable if you are smart and stay within your capabilities and preferences. But do not be afraid to break the rules. Or, make up your own rules and do what you feel most comfortable with. And do not hesitate to make use of the local delicatessen or traiteur – offering guests your favourite take-away foods plus a few home-made dishes should be no reason for guilt.

Make the best of all that is in season too, for reasons of taste and economy. Budget must be a major factor when planning a menu as, ultimately, it will affect what you can and cannot afford to

serve. Generally, the more choice you offer, the more it is going to cost you. So, if you are feeling particularly poor, why not just serve one great soup, a hunk of rustic bread and a single, perfectly ripe cheese. That is not in the chart, but didn't I just say 'break the rules'? Remember, the chart is simply a guideline to give you a helping hand.

Calculating quantities

Calculating quantities of food for a party is never an easy thing to do. A lot depends on the type of party, who is coming, the time of day and many other factors.

Determining quantities for buffets when there is a large choice is probably the most difficult. Generally, the more people you are feeding, the less you will need to allow per head. You have to assume that everyone will have a little of everything, but not knowing which dish will be the popular one means you have to allow extra to compensate.

A useful tip if you are unsure is to take out the serving dishes you plan to use and think, for example, 'That will serve ten people.' Then, when you go shopping, you can visualize the amounts needed to fill that dish. Remember that it is always better to have too much than too little and you can always eat it the following day. As for the range of dishes you should offer, I strongly believe that less is best. Fewer dishes make more impact on the table and on the plate. It will also strain your budget and resources less. The chart overleaf will help you calculate quantities.

Advance preparation

Freezing prepared food for parties has lots of advantages. It means that if you know that time is going to be tight on the day of

When you know time will be scarce on the day of the party, choose a menu for which most of the dishes can be prepared in advance and frozen. Regular hosts can even double the quantities of recipes and freeze in batches to save more time.

the event, and you choose your recipes well, you can get ahead by freezing the bulk of the menu, or certainly some of the component parts. If you are a regular party giver, double up on your favourite recipes and freeze them to save time, energy and expense, particularly with seasonal foods. The freezer is also a real asset for party leftovers, as long as they have not been previously frozen.

Most foods freeze well, but for best results, it is important to freeze them quickly. Make sure that hot dishes are completely cold before you wrap and freeze them. Use plastic freezer bags, foil bags, lidded foil containers and sturdy plastic freezer containers with lids to store foods and to prevent any 'freezer burn'. Freeze liquids, such as soups, sauces and drinks, in freezer bags placed in square containers. Then freeze them until solid, turn out and return to the freezer. It is

Food quantities

FINGER FOODS

The following amounts are per person

Canapés
● Allow 4 to 6 bite-sized canapés for each hour that the party will last.
● If guests are going to be at the party for more than 3 hours, offer something more substantial, like bruschetta, to eat towards the end, since canapés are never a substitute for a full meal.

Finger buffet
● Allow 8 to 12 substantial finger food items, if it is a substitute for a meal.

FORK FOODS

The following amounts are per person

Poultry, meat and fish *trimmed/boned weight*
● 6oz/175g when you only have 1 main dish
● 8oz/225g when you have more than 2 or 3 main dishes. For example, if you were serving chicken and fish you would allow 4oz/110g of each, and if you were serving 3 dishes you would allow 3oz/75g of each
● 2½oz/60g poultry, meat or fish, 2oz/50g rice, grains, lentils, pasta or noodles and 2oz/50g vegetables for a single main course one-pot dish

Potatoes *unpeeled weight*
● 4oz/110g new potatoes (if leaving skins on), or 6oz/175g old potatoes, to accompany a single main course
● 3oz/75g new potatoes (if leaving skins on), or 4½oz/125g old potatoes, when 2 to 3 main courses and salads or vegetables are being served

Vegetables *prepared weight*
● 4oz/110g for most vegetables, unless they have a lot of stalk or need a lot of peeling, such as root vegetables, when you would need to double the amount, to accompany a single main course
● 2oz/50g when 2 to 3 main courses and salads or vegetables are being served

Rice, grains and lentils *uncooked weight*
● 1½oz/40g rice, grains or lentils to accompany a single fish, meat or poultry main course
● 1½oz/40g rice for a first course risotto
● 2oz/50g rice for a main course risotto
● 1oz/25g rice, grains or lentils when 2 to 3 main courses and salads or vegetables are being served
● 2oz/50g rice, grains or lentils, 2½oz/65g poultry, meat or fish and 2oz/50g vegetables for a single main course one-pot dish

Beans *uncooked weight*
● 2½oz/60g to accompany a single fish, meat or poultry main course
● 1oz/25g when 2 or 3 main courses and salads or vegetables are being served

Pasta and noodles *uncooked weight*
● 3oz/75g for a first course
● 4oz/110g for a single main course
● 2oz/50g to accompany a single main course
● 1oz/25g when 2 to 3 main courses, salads or vegetables are being served

Leaf Salads
● 1oz/25g unprepared weight, or ½oz/15g prepared weight mixed salad leaves, to accompany a first course, main course, buffet or cheese course

Butter
● ½oz/15g to serve with bread or crackers and cheese

Cheese
● 4oz/110g if serving on its own, or 2oz/50g when you are serving a pudding as well

Desserts
● 5oz/150g prepared weight fruit
● A generous slice of pastries, tarts and cakes
● 4oz/110g mousses and creamy desserts
● 5floz/150ml ice-creams and sorbets
● When you are serving two desserts – such as a fruit dish and a mousse – allow slightly more than half the total quantities of each. For example, 4oz/110g fruit and 3oz/75g mousse

important that meat, poultry and fish are defrosted in the fridge to prevent the growth of any harmful bacteria, but most other foods can be defrosted at room temperature, out of sunlight. Refer to the individual recipes in this book for details of how long to freeze particular dishes and how best to reheat or complete them.

Serving

When you are inviting lots of people over, you should consider having buffet tables at both ends of the room to avoid everyone congregating in one place. Make sure, though, that wherever you site these tables, there is an easy route to bring food through from the kitchen. If you have the space, allow a separate table for the dessert, plates and cutlery and put it all out in advance of the meal. People eat at different speeds and you may find that some of them are ready to move on to the dessert whilst others are still tucking into their main course. Never put a buffet table and a bar table next to each other as you will find that this arrangement will cause a major bottleneck.

If time, or space, is tight, there are occasions when I do not set up a buffet table at all. Instead, I individually plate all the food in the kitchen and, if I am serving two or three main courses, I send out a selection of them on very large trays. The waiting staff make sure that each tray has a good range of dishes on it so that there is something for everyone, with a meat, a fish and a vegetarian option. Forks get put on to the sides of plates and napkins all get piled in the centre of the tray.

When you are using buffet tables, set out plates, cutlery and the same array of food at the start, middle and end of the

table to avoid bottlenecks and delays. To prevent your guests from needlessly queuing at the buffet table, do not make a big announcement that the food is ready. Instead, invite small groups of people, say ten at a time, to come up to the table and get their food. I always like to have some help serving buffet dishes as it means you can control the amount of food being served (particularly useful for occasions when you have accidentally under-catered) and these helpers can keep relays of dishes coming from the kitchen so that the food is hot for everyone.

If you are planning to have a seated fork buffet, often a cold first course can be plated in advance and put on the table

Cocktail parties are a marvellous way to show off your individual style if you choose decorations and serving dishes to suit. This is an amusing yet practical way to offer round small cones of fish and chips, invariably a popular choice of canapé.

just before everyone sits down to the meal. Guests can then come up to the buffet table and help themselves to the main course and, later on, to the dessert. Alternatively, the pudding can be plated and then served by helpers, if you do not want your friends bobbing up and down too much during the meal.

At a stand up buffet, I sometimes go around with platters of food in case anyone is ravenous and wants a second helping, which saves them having to return to the table to get it themselves.

Finger food only

English Drinks Party Menu

- Radishes with Watercress Butter *p42*
- Cheddar Scones with Mustard
  Butter & Ham *p48*
- Sausage & Mash Croustades *p50*
- Quail Egg & Smoked Salmon Tartlets *p57*
- Fish & Chips *p74*
- Whisky Sour *p154*

Saffron mussels in garlic bread

Fish & chips

Mediterranean Drinks Party Menu

- Celery with Olive & Parsley Salad *p42*
- Cheddar Crackers, Goat Cheese, Tomatoes
  & Basil *p56*
- Camembert Ice-Cream on Parmesan
  Toasts *p53*
- Saffron Mussels in Garlic Bread *p53*
- Deep-Fried Sage Leaves with Anchovies *p74*
- Italian Vegetable Skewers *p76*
- Negroni *p157*

Fork food only

Family Lunch Menu

- Courgette & Seafood Salad *p100*
- Chicken Scaloppine with Mozzarella
  & Sage *p97*
- Roasted Vegetables *p130*
  omit the roasted tomatoes
- Baked Peaches with Figs, Ginger &
  Spices *p132*

Baked peaches with figs, ginger & spices

suggested menus

Here are a few themed menus to get you thinking about what food and drinks you might like to serve at your party. You can follow them closely, or use them as a base and add your own ideas, bearing in mind the rules of good menu planning mentioned on page 23. More delicious menus can be found on the feature pages in the recipe chapters of this book.

Children's Birthday Party Menu

- Garlic Potato Crisps *p39*
- Hamburgers *p48*
- Sausages & Parsley Mash *p36*
- Fish & Chips *p74*
- Vermicelli Prawns on Chinese Seaweed *p74*
- Yogurt Ices *p83*
- Happy Birthday Cup Cakes *p85*
- Lime, Orange & Lemon Citrus Pressé *p148*

Yogurt ices

Courgette & seafood salad

Do-Ahead Menu

- Saffron Lamb Tagine with Couscous *p95*
- Rocket, French Bean, Red Onion & Croûton Salad *p128*
- Apricot Tart *p135*

One-Hour Menu

- Thai Mussels *p102*
- Green Salad *p126*
- Saffron Cream with Sesame-Poppy Seed Wafers *p137*

Thai mussels

Wedding Menu

- Roast Beef Salad *p95*
- Courgette & Seafood Salad *p100*
- Chicken Tonnato Salad *p96*
- Taboulleh Primavera *p112*
- Potato, Watercress & Walnut Salad *p129*
- Tomato Salad *p126*
- Rolled Pavlova with Mango & Passionfruit *p133*
- Red Berry Kissel with Biscotti & Vanilla Cream *p132*
- Heart Cake with Rosepetals *p141*
- Long Island Iced Tea *p154*
- Limey *p149*

Mozzarella salad with olives, anchovies & parsley

Vegetarian Special Occasion Menu

- Green Mango & Papaya Salad *p127*
- Asian Ravioli with Soy-Butter Sauce *p118*
- Stir-fried Bok Choy, Asparagus & Sugar Snaps *p130*
- Lime & Pistachio Kulfi with Pistachio Wafers *p139*
- Simply Red *p157*

Finger and fork food

All-American Menu

- Chicory with Roquefort, Pecans & Cranberries *p42*
- Cornmeal Muffins with Maryland Crab Cakes *p51*
- Jambalaya *p116*
- Green Salad *p126*
- Tomato Salad *p126*
- Apple & Blackberry Filo Pastries *p134*
- Mint Julep *p154*

Chicory with roquefort, pecans & cranberries

Glamorous Menu

- Caviar Eclairs *p55*
- Quail Egg & Smoked Salmon Tartlets *p57*
- Brioche filled with Wild Mushrooms *p53*
- Seared Salmon, Asparagus & Potato Salad *p100*
- Cucumber, Sugar Snap & Radish Salad *p126*
- Borlotti & Green Beans *p131*
- Raspberry & Lemon Syllabub Trifle *p136*
- Champagne & Sorbet Fizz *p154*

Light & Healthy Menu

- Vietnamese Chicken Salad *p96*
  omit the Chinese leaves or Napa cabbage
- Mozzarella with Olives, Anchovies & Parsley *p129*
- Oriental Coleslaw *p127*
- Elderflower Jellies *p78*
- Kiwi Cooler *p152*

At parties, drinks deserve as much attention as food. For some, it might just be a well-chosen wine, a few icy cold beers or a fabulous fruity cocktail. These days, apart from making sure that everyone is happily taken care of, there are no rigid rules about what you should and should not serve. However, there will be some occasions when you want to offer a wider range of drinks, so refer to the charts on these pages. They will help you plan the quantities, chilling and bar equipment needed.

Whatever drinks you decide to serve at the party, keep them simple. People do not want to be offered a vast array of refreshments and, apart from that, you will find it expensive and demanding to provide a fully stocked bar.

The starting point should be the type of party you are having and the drinking habits of your guests. There could be young, old, teetotallers, those who insist on their favourite tipple and others who are content to drink anything on offer.

To set up a bar, you ideally need a 5ft10in/1.78m long table or counter for each 50 to 75 guests. Protect any precious surfaces by covering them with plastic wrap before putting down the tablecloth. Then put plastic sheeting beneath the table to protect the floor.

If you do not have a large enough fridge to chill all your drinks, you will

	20 GUESTS		40 GUESTS		60 GUESTS		
	2 hours	3 hours	2 hours	3 hours	2 hours	3 hours	
CHAMPAGNE PARTY							
Champagne/ Sparkling wine	9 x 750ml bottles	14 x 750ml bottles	17 x 750ml bottles	27 x 750ml bottles	25 x 750ml bottles	40 x 750ml bottles	Finger food party
WINE PARTY							
White wine	7 x 750ml bottles	11 x 750ml bottles	16 x 750ml bottles	22 x 750ml bottles	20 x 750ml bottles	32 x 750ml bottles	
Red wine	3 x 750ml bottles	5 x 750ml bottles	6 x 750ml bottles	10 x 750ml bottles	10 x 750ml bottles	16 x 750ml bottles	
CHAMPAGNE OR WINE PARTY							
Soft drinks	3.5 litres	6 litres	7 litres	11 litres	14 litres	18 litres	
Mineral water	5 litres	8 litres	10 litres	15 litres	15 litres	22 litres	

	20 GUESTS	40 GUESTS	60 GUESTS	
WINE PARTY				
White wine	8 x 750ml bottles	16 x 750ml bottles	24 x 750ml bottles	Fork food party
Red wine	4 x 750ml bottles	8 x 750ml bottles	12 x 750ml bottles	
Soft drinks	3.5 litres	7 litres	14 litres	
Mineral water	7 litres	14 litres	20 litres	

need to allow 1lb/450g ice per person, which is enough for chilling bottles and for adding to drinks. On very hot days, or if the party is going to go on for many hours, allow more. Chill everything in a clean dustbin or similar deep waterproof container which will take 31lb/14kg of ice and about 36 bottles. Put this on the plastic sheeting, along with a bin for empties. Layer up the bottles with ice and add some cold water, particularly if you are in a hurry, to speed the chilling process, which will take about an hour.

To save time later when serving, open still wines, push the cork back into the bottle and chill. If you are having a large party, try to chill the drinks in separate containers as you will find it faster to dispense them. Store ice for putting into drinks in a separate ice-bucket to avoid contamination. Make crushed ice by putting ice-cubes in a clean dish towel and hitting them with a rolling pin.

You will need twice as many glasses as people as they get abandoned easily. Choose the glass to match the drink: flutes for champagne; a generous wine glass for wines, juice and water; straight-sided highballs for long drinks served with ice; tumblers for spirits and juices; v-shaped glasses for cocktails; balloon glasses for brandy. In the end though, unless hiring glasses, we all make do with what we have. You can get away with just champagne and wine glasses.

Ideally, for a bar for 50 guests, you will also need five drinks trays, an ice bucket, a wine cooler, three jugs, a bowl for garnishes and six waiters' napkins. Make sure you have the equipment listed in the checklist on page 21 too. Scale the quantities of equipment up or down according to the number of guests.

Calculating quantities

Champagne or sparkling wine:
There are 6 champagne flutes to a 750ml bottle. For a 2 hour drinks party, if the only other drinks you are serving are mineral water and soft drinks, allow 2½ glasses each. As an aperitif before dinner, allow 1½ glasses per person. At weddings, when you want to toast the bride and groom, a single glass each is sufficient. A single glass is also enough to serve with dessert. When you are diluting champagne or sparkling wine with a fruit purée, allow about 8 glasses per bottle.

Wines:
There are about 5 medium wine glasses to a 750ml bottle. For a 2 hour drinks party, if you are not serving anything else, apart from mineral water and soft drinks, allow 1 bottle for 2 people. At drinks parties, white wine is generally more popular than red so have two-thirds white to one-third red. For fork lunches or suppers, allow 2 glasses of white wine and 1½ glasses of red each. If you are providing only red or white, 3 glasses will generally be enough.

Spirits and Mixers:
A 700ml bottle will make about 17 single measures, served in old-fashioned tumblers. If you are only serving spirits or cocktails, mineral water and juice at a 2 hour drinks party, you probably need to allow 3 per person. The range of spirits to offer is purely personal, but these days it is more usual to find a basic bar of gin, whisky and vodka, as well as wines and beers, rather than a fully stocked bar. However, if you do want a fuller bar you could add tequila, brandy, Campari, rum, bourbon, vermouth and sherry.

The obligatory mixers are orange juice, soda, tonic, dry ginger ale, tomato juice and cola. Do not forget to provide lemons for mixing and slicing, any other garnishes and bottles of Tabasco and Worcestershire sauce for pepping up tomato juice.

Liqueurs:
A 700ml bottle of liqueur, such as armagnac, other brandy, Cointreau or similar, will give about 15 liqueur or brandy glasses for an after dinner drink. You should only need 1 per person.

Mineral water:
Each 1¾ pint/1 litre [1 quart] bottle yields about 5 glasses. For a 2 hour drinks party, provide 1 bottle for every 4 guests. Remember that some will prefer still water to sparkling so you will need to allow an appropriate amount. For a fork lunch or supper, a bottle between 3 will be enough.

Soft drinks:
At a 2 hour drinks party, when you are serving champagne or wine, along with mineral water, you need to allow some soft drinks. A glass, or about 6floz/175ml of juice each, will do. But for parties at which you are only going to serve soft drinks and no alcohol whatsoever, allow a total of about 3 glasses each.

finger

Whether it is a **few snacks** for a casual party with friends or a stunning **style statement**, accompanied by fine wines, **spirits** and your best frock or suit, here you'll find **all you need** to know about producing **great nibbles**. Inspiration comes from the **food jet-set**, with fresh flavours flown in from the **Far East**, Americas, Europe and the Med. We start at the very beginning, with **really easy** dishes requiring **no cooking** and antipasto ideas more about **good shopping** than **chef-class** cookery techniques. But for those times when you want to show off, there is also a selection of **eye-opening**, mouth-dropping, lip-smacking **canapés with wit**. Not sure how to put it all together? The **feature** pages have stylish ideas for **romantic** weddings, **informal** housewarmings and **classy** cocktail dos. Easy on the cook, delicious on the guests, this food is **finger-licking** fantastic.

FOOD

Olives, feta & chillies

A colourful array of Mediterranean ingredients that takes a matter of minutes to assemble. SERVES 10

12oz/350g [1½ cups] mixed olives
  such as black niçoise, purple kalamata
  & green stuffed with almonds
4oz/110g feta, broken into pieces
1oz/25g pickled hot chillies
A few basil leaves

Toss all the ingredients together in a bowl and serve.

Advance preparation: assemble up to 5 hours ahead, adding the basil just before serving.
Freezing: not suitable.

Spoon canapés

The perfect way to serve prime ingredients and show off any pretty or unusual spoons that you have. MAKES 30

for the crab & lemon
4oz/110g [1 cup] fresh white crab meat
2 tsp lemon juice
1 spring onion [scallion], finely sliced
Salt
for the gingered oysters
10 oysters
2 tblsp rice wine or white wine vinegar
2in/5cm piece ginger, cut into fine strips
for the caviar & crème fraîche
3oz/75g [⅓ cup] crème fraîche
2oz/50g Sevruga caviar
You will also need 30 spoons

Season the crab meat with the lemon juice and salt. Arrange it on 10 of the spoons and garnish with the spring onion.
Divide the oysters amongst 10 spoons and sprinkle with the vinegar and ginger.
Place the crème fraîche on the remaining spoons and top with the caviar.
Arrange them all on a platter and serve.

Advance preparation: cut the spring onion and ginger up to 8 hours before,

left Olives, feta & chillies

cover and chill. Arrange the ingredients on the spoons up to 30 minutes before, cover and keep chilled.
Freezing: not suitable.

Bagel crisps & pink peppercorn gravadlax

Pink peppercorns give the salmon a splash of colour and a touch of heat. MAKES 10

4oz/110g gravadlax, sliced
10 bagel crisps
2 tsp dried pink peppercorns, crushed
2 limes, halved lengthways

Cut the gravadlax into 10 pieces and arrange them in rosettes on the bagels.
Scatter over the peppercorns and serve with the limes for guests to squeeze.

Advance preparation: top the bagels and cut the limes up to 1 hour ahead. Cover and chill.
Freezing: not suitable.

Vodka cherry tomatoes with herbed garlic salt

Add the leftover vodka marinade to a jug of Bloody Mary or some Oyster Shooters (page 156). The garlic salt will keep for ages in a screw-topped jar and is terrific sprinkled on meat, fish, poultry and vegetables before grilling or roasting. SERVES 10

for the vodka tomatoes
8oz/225g red & yellow cherry tomatoes
5floz/150ml vodka
1 tblsp Worcestershire sauce
12 drops Tabasco sauce
1 medium clove garlic, crushed
for the herbed garlic salt
2oz/50g [⅓ cup] Maldon or flaked sea salt
Grated zest of ½ lemon
1 tsp black peppercorns, crushed
1 rounded tsp chopped rosemary
1 small clove garlic, crushed

Cut a small cross in the base of each tomato and place in a bowl.
Stir the vodka, the Worcestershire and Tabasco sauces and the garlic into the

bowl of tomatoes. Cover and marinate in the fridge for 24 hours.
Mix all the ingredients together for the herbed garlic salt and leave to infuse for at least 2 hours.
Drain the tomatoes, reserving the liquid for another recipe. Serve with the flavoured salt to dip.

Advance preparation: the tomatoes can be marinated 2 days in advance; the herbed salt can be made weeks ahead.
Freezing: not suitable.

Prawn crackers & Chinese salsa

This is a ten minute recipe for when you are in a real hurry. SERVES 10

20 prawn crackers, or root vegetable crisps [chips]
for the Chinese salsa
1 tsp finely grated ginger
1 tblsp light soy sauce
1 tblsp toasted sesame seeds
¼ green sweet pepper, roughly chopped
¼ yellow sweet pepper, roughly chopped
1 red bird's-eye chilli, seeded & finely chopped
1 tblsp toasted sesame oil

Mix all the salsa ingredients together to make a wet paste and serve in a bowl alongside the crackers for guests to dip.

Spoon canapés

Advance preparation: make the salsa up to 4 hours before, cover and keep cool.
Freezing: not suitable.

Rice crackers with crispy vegetables

I also like to top Japanese rice crackers with prawns or shrimps and a dollop of plain yogurt flavoured with some ground cumin and coriander. MAKES 10

10 Japanese rice cracker discs
for the vegetables
¼ small red sweet pepper, finely sliced
¼ small yellow sweet pepper, finely sliced
1 small carrot, finely sliced
3 mangetout [snow peas], finely sliced
A few shiso leaves, to garnish
for the dressing
1 tsp rice wine vinegar
A pinch of salt
A pinch of sugar
3 drops Tabasco sauce

Mix the sliced vegetables in a bowl with the vinegar, salt, sugar and Tabasco.
Spoon onto the rice crackers and garnish with the shiso leaves. Serve them within 30 minutes of topping.

Advance preparation: cut the vegetables 1 day before and store separately in the fridge in plastic wrap.
Freezing: not suitable.

Mediterranean antipasto

What could be simpler than an assortment of everyday Mediterranean ingredients presented on a platter? Include a selection of salamis, one fine textured, one coarse and another hot and spicy. A pot of rillettes, or thick slice of pâté, would not go amiss here, served with some good bread. SERVES 10

20 slices mixed salamis, such as Felino, Milano, Calabrese & Soppressata
10 bocconcini (tiny mozzarella)
8oz/225g [about 1 cup] drained bottled char-grilled artichokes in oil
5oz/150g radishes
2oz/50g [⅓ cup] caperberries
5oz/150g [1 cup] olives

Arrange the antipasto ingredients on a platter and serve.

Advance preparation: arrange up to 4 hours ahead, cover and chill.
Freezing: not suitable.

Asian antipasto

Fill the tomatoes with basil pesto if you prefer. Crispy Duck Pancakes (page 41), made without chives, are a good addition to this platter, as are quail eggs (page 36), dipped into the Szechwan salt. SERVES 10

5oz/150g Thai or other asparagus
10 large cooked prawns or shrimps, peeled
for the coriander roasted tomatoes
5 plum tomatoes, halved lengthways
2 tblsp olive oil
A large pinch of sugar
1 x Coriander Pesto Recipe (page 43), or 3oz/75g [⅓ cup] ready-made pesto
Salt & freshly ground black pepper
for the gingered mushrooms
3 tblsp toasted sesame oil
5oz/150g fresh shiitake mushrooms
1 tsp finely grated ginger
for the Szechwan salt
1½ tblsp flaked sea salt
1 tsp Szechwan peppercorns, seeded

for the won-tons
Vegetable oil, for deep-frying
10 won-ton wrappers
A pinch of salt
½ tsp five-spice powder
A large and small square of banana leaf, to serve, optional

Heat the oven to 190°C/375°F/Gas 5. Seed the tomatoes and put them skin-side down in a roasting pan. Drizzle with oil and sprinkle with sugar, salt and pepper.
Roast the tomatoes for 30 minutes or until soft and slightly charred. Remove from the pan whilst warm, lift onto paper towels, cool and top them with the pesto.
Boil the asparagus for 2-3 minutes in a pan of salted water until al dente. Drain under cold water and dry on paper towels.
Heat the sesame oil in a pan. Sauté the mushrooms and ginger for 3-4 minutes. Drain, cool and season with salt.
Stir the sea salt and Szechwan peppercorns over a medium heat for 1 minute or

Mediterranean antipasto

until smoking. Cool, grind briefly and place on a small square of banana leaf, or in a bowl, to dip the prawns.

Heat the vegetable oil in a large pan to 350°F/180°C. Fry the won-ton wrappers for 30 seconds until golden, drain and cool. Dust with the salt and five-spice.

Arrange everything on a plate lined with a large square of banana leaf and serve.

Advance preparation: 2 days before, make the Szechwan salt and store in an airtight jar; roast the tomatoes, cool and chill. Cook the asparagus and mushrooms 1 day before, cover and chill. Fry the won-ton wrappers 12 hours before and store in an airtight box. Fill the tomatoes and assemble the platter 1 hour before. *Freezing: not suitable.*

Middle Eastern antipasto

Dukkah is an Egyptian mixture of crushed nuts and spices. Dip the flatbread into the oil and then into the dukkah. SERVES 10

1 x Moroccan Meatballs Recipe (page 40)
1 x Sesame Cheese Straws Recipe
　(page 54)
1 x Olives, Feta & Chillies Recipe (page 32)
3floz/75ml olive oil
2 large sheets Lebanese flatbread, torn
for the dukkah
2oz/50g [⅓ cup] almonds or hazelnuts
4oz/110g [¾ cup] white sesame seeds
1oz/25g [¼ cup] coriander seeds
1oz/25g [¼ cup] cumin seeds
Salt & freshly ground black pepper

Dry-fry the nuts and spices over a high heat for 1 minute, stirring constantly.

Crush the nuts and spices, then season.

Arrange the dukkah in a bowl on a platter with a bowl of oil for dipping the flatbread, plus the assembled dishes of meatballs, sesame biscuits and olives.

Advance preparation: roast the nuts and spices 4 hours ahead and cover. Assemble the platter 1 hour before serving. *Freezing: not suitable*

right Asian antipasto

Quail eggs with roasted sesame salt

You have to like your friends a lot to peel quail eggs for them! SERVES 10

36 quail eggs
1 rounded tblsp white sesame seeds
A pinch of cayenne pepper
A pinch of cumin
1 rounded tblsp Maldon or flaked sea salt
A pinch of ground black pepper

Put the eggs into a pan of boiling water. Boil for 2 minutes 45 seconds for soft-boiled, 3 minutes for hard-boiled. Drain under running cold water until stone cold.
Reserve a few eggs in their shells to garnish. Peel the rest, rinse, dry on paper towels and put into a serving dish.
Dry-fry the remaining ingredients over a low heat for 2-3 minutes. Cool, put into a small dish and serve with the quail eggs.

Advance preparation: make the salt dip 1 week ahead and store in an airtight jar. Cook and peel the eggs 1 day before, cover and chill.
Freezing: not suitable.

Sausages & parsley mash

Make this old-fashioned favourite for lunch or supper as well as drinks parties. SERVES 10

1lb/450g pork cocktail sausages
2 tblsp vegetable oil
for the parsley mash
1lb/450g boiling potatoes, quartered
1½oz/40g flat-leaved parsley
3 tblsp olive oil
2 tblsp double cream

Cook the potatoes in a pan of salted water for 15-20 minutes until tender. Drain and mash until smooth.
Heat the olive oil and cream in a pan to just below boiling point then pour into a food processor with the parsley. Blend until the parsley is roughly chopped.
Stir the parsley mixture into the potato purée, season well and cover with foil.
Heat the oven to 375°F/190°C/Gas 5. Roast the sausages in the vegetable oil for

20-25 minutes until brown. Reheat the mash in the oven for 15 minutes.
Drain the sausages on paper towels and serve with the parsley mash as a dip.

Advance preparation: make the parsley mash 2 days before, cover and chill.
Freezing: freeze the mash 4 weeks before.

Bean brandade crudités

This garlicky bean brandade can also be used as a bruschetta topping. SERVES 10

for the bean brandade
8oz/225g [1½ cups] drained canned
  cannellini beans
1 large clove garlic, crushed
2 tblsp lemon juice

Quail eggs with roasted sesame salt

8 tblsp olive oil
2 tblsp double cream [heavy cream]
2 tblsp roughly chopped parsley
Salt & freshly ground black pepper
for the crudités
5floz/150ml white wine
1 small clove garlic, crushed
8oz/225g small fresh mussels
1lb/450g small clams
2 heads red or yellow chicory
1 head trevise or radicchio
2 heads dandelion greens
10 baby fennel bulbs
1lb/450g small carrots
8oz/225g rapini or other broccoli

Reserve a third of the beans. Purée the rest in a processor with the garlic, lemon juice, oil, cream, parsley and seasoning.

Add the reserved beans and pulse until roughly chopped and combined with the rest of the mixture. Transfer to a bowl.
Heat the wine and garlic in a large pan over a high heat, add the mussels and clams, cover and steam for 4-5 minutes until all the shells have opened. Discard any that are unopened. Remove with a slotted spoon and cool.
Separate the salad leaves and arrange them with the vegetables and shellfish on a platter with the brandade.

Advance preparation: make the bean brandade up to 3 days ahead, cover and chill. Steam the shellfish up to 6 hours before, cover and chill. Assemble up to 4 hours ahead, cover and chill.
Freezing: not suitable.

Grissini & rouille dip

Rouille also makes a vibrant dressing for chicken salads or pasta. SERVES 10

for the grissini
4oz/110g strong plain flour [1 cup all-purpose flour], sifted + extra for rolling
¼oz/7g easy blend yeast [1 pkg rapid-rise dry yeast]
A pinch of salt
3 tblsp warm water
1 tblsp olive oil + extra for greasing
1 tblsp roughly chopped parsley
2 tblsp roughly chopped black olives
2 tsp finely chopped hot red chillies
1 tsp flaked sea salt
for the rouille
2oz/50g white bread, crusts removed
4½ tblsp olive oil
15oz/425g [2 cups] drained, rinsed canned pimientos, roughly chopped
2 cloves garlic, crushed
Salt & freshly ground black pepper

Mix the flour, yeast and salt together. Stir in the water and oil to make a soft dough, adding more water if needed.
Knead for 5 minutes until smooth. Place in a bowl, cover and leave in a warm place for 1 hour or until doubled in size.
Divide the dough into 4 and add the parsley to one quarter, olives to another, chilli to the third and leave the last plain.
Knead to incorporate the flavourings and divide each of the doughs into 5.
Heat the oven to 375°F/190°C/Gas 5. Roll each batch of dough out on a lightly floured surface and cut them thinly into 8-10in/20-25.5cm long grissini. Sprinkle the salt over the final unflavoured batch.
Place on lightly oiled baking trays and bake for 8-10 minutes until crisp and golden. Remove to a wire rack to cool.
Soak the bread for the rouille in the oil for 10 minutes. Purée the pimientos and garlic in a processor. Gradually add the soaked bread and blend until smooth. Season and serve in a bowl with the grissini to dip.

Advance preparation: make the rouille up to 2 days before, cover and chill.
Freezing: make and freeze the grissini up to 4 weeks before.

Masala potato wedges

The heat of these spicy potatoes is balanced by a fruity tamarind ketchup. SERVES 10

for the masala potato wedges
4 tblsp water
4 tblsp tomato paste
4 tblsp lemon juice
½ tsp hot chilli powder
1 tblsp ground coriander
2 tsp ground cumin
2 tsp salt
4 tblsp vegetable oil
5 medium potatoes, unpeeled & cut lengthways into 6
for the Indian ketchup
1 tsp brown mustard seeds
1 tblsp toasted sesame oil
2 cloves garlic, crushed
½ tsp ground cardamom
½ tsp finely grated ginger
A pinch of ground cinnamon
A pinch of ground cloves
½ tsp cayenne
2oz/50g [¼ cup] dark brown sugar
½ tsp salt
1oz/25g concentrated tamarind paste
1lb/450g canned chopped tomatoes

Heat the oven to 350°F/180°C/Gas 4. Whisk the water, tomato paste, lemon juice, spices and salt to a paste.
Pour the oil into a roasting pan, add the potatoes, then spoon over the paste and stir to coat well. Bake for 25 minutes until cooked through and dark golden, shaking the potatoes from time to time.
Fry the mustard seeds for the ketchup in the sesame oil over a medium heat for about 30 seconds. Lower the heat and stir in the garlic, all the spices, sugar and salt. Cook for 1 minute, stirring.
Add the tamarind and tomatoes. Simmer for 10-15 minutes until thick.
Cool the ketchup then spoon it into a serving bowl. Serve the hot potato wedges with the ketchup to dip.

Advance preparation: make the ketchup up to 5 days before, cover and chill.
Freezing: freeze the ketchup up to 4 weeks before. Simmer for 5 minutes if it needs thickening after being defrosted.

Poppadoms & chutneys

I like to supplement ordinary shop-bought poppadoms with some different varieties from my favourite Indian restaurant, such as the flower-like achappams and pappadavadai, which are dipped in a spiced rice flour batter. If you do want to make your own dip, the Indian ketchup (page 35) is an authentic partner. SERVES 10

2 x 8oz/225g jars Indian chutneys or
    pickles, such as mango, lime or
    aubergine [eggplant]
Vegetable oil, for deep-frying
20 spiced poppadoms

Spoon the chutneys or pickles into bowls.
Heat the oil in a deep-fat fryer or large pan to 350°F/180°C. Fry the poppadoms one at a time in the oil for 30-40 seconds or until crisp and golden. Drain on paper towels. Alternatively, toast them under a preheated grill [broiler] on both sides for about 20-30 seconds in total, until puffy. Serve hot or cold with the chutneys.

Advance preparation: cook the poppadoms 1 day ahead and store in an airtight box. Reheat in a warm oven.
Freezing: not suitable

Garlic potato crisps

Potato crisps are addictive enough, but tossing them in hot garlic butter makes them even more so. Since they will disappear in a flash, make more than you could possibly imagine your friends eating. SERVES 10

1¼lb/570g potato crisps [potato chips]
for the garlic butter
5oz/150g [10 tblsp] butter
1 large clove garlic, crushed
2 rounded tblsp chopped parsley
Salt & freshly ground black pepper

Put the crisps into a shallow ovenproof dish or baking tray.
Melt the butter, add the garlic and cook over a low heat for 30 seconds, then add

left Vietnamese rice crackers with peanut sauce

lots of salt and some pepper. Cool a little, stir in the parsley, pour over the crisps and toss so that they are well coated.
Heat through for 3-5 minutes in an oven set to 350°F/180°C/Gas 4 and serve.

Advance preparation: the crisps can be tossed in the garlic butter up to 1 day ahead, stored in an airtight container and kept in a cool place. Heat as above.
Freezing: make the garlic-parsley butter and freeze up to 4 weeks before.

Lacquered sesame nuts

This recipe is adapted from the one in Yan Kit-So's excellent book Classic Food of China. *I've added unlacquered macadamias and pistachios for variety.* SERVES 10

9oz/250g [2 cups] cashew nuts
1½oz/40g [3 tblsp] sugar
4½oz/125g golden syrup [6 tblsp light
    corn syrup]
Vegetable oil, for deep-frying
2 tsp roasted white sesame seeds
3oz/75g [¾ cup] macadamia nuts
3oz/75g [¾ cup] peeled pistachio nuts
You will also need a cooking thermometer

Put the cashews in a saucepan, cover with water and boil for 5 minutes, skimming as necessary. Drain.
Return the cashews to the pan, pour over 2½ pints/1.5 litres [1½ quarts] of boiling water, add the sugar and boil 5 minutes, stirring occasionally. Drain again.
Heat the same pan for 1 minute until hot, then remove it from the heat and add the still-hot cashew nuts and the golden syrup. Mix well to glaze every nut.
Put the pan back onto a medium heat and stir for 20-30 seconds before pouring the cashew nuts into a colander to drain off all the excess syrup.
Half-fill a medium-sized pan or wok with oil and heat to 350°F/180°C. Carefully spoon the cashews into the hot oil, which will foam. Stir gently with a slotted spoon from time to time, frying for 7-8 minutes until golden brown.
Remove the cashews with the slotted spoon, drain in a colander and sprinkle

over the sesame seeds. Shake to separate the nuts before they cool and harden.
Toss the cold lacquered cashews with the macadamias and pistachios and serve.

Advance preparation: make the lacquered cashews up to 2 weeks ahead and store in a cool place in an air-tight box lined with baking parchment.
Freezing: not suitable

Vietnamese rice crackers with peanut sauce

In Vietnam, banh trang are normally moistened and used for spring rolls. Here they are deep-fried and served with a spicy peanut sauce also used in the bruschetta section as a sauce for chicken. SERVES 10

Vegetable oil, for deep-frying
20 rice paper wrappers (banh trang)
for the peanut sauce
1 tblsp light soy sauce
1 tblsp toasted sesame oil
1 tblsp lemon juice
1 tblsp clear honey
1 tblsp finely grated ginger
3 rounded tblsp crunchy peanut butter
1 small red bird's-eye chilli, seeded &
    finely diced
1 small clove garlic, crushed
4 tblsp boiling water
1 tblsp peanuts, roughly chopped

Put all the sauce ingredients, except for half the chilli and the peanuts, into a food processor and pulse 7-8 times to blend.
Spoon into a bowl and scatter over the remaining chilli and the peanuts.
Heat the oil in a deep-fat fryer or large pan to 350°F/180°C. Fry the rice paper wrappers one at a time in the hot oil for 30-40 seconds until crisp and golden.
Drain on paper towels. Serve hot or cold with the peanut dipping sauce.

Advance preparation: make the sauce 2 weeks ahead, cover and chill. Cook the crackers 1 day in advance and store in an airtight box. Crisp up in a warm oven.
Freezing: make and freeze the sauce up to 4 weeks before.

Lebanese bread, hummous & vegetables

This is a very fast wrap to make. Tzatziki is good used in place of hummous. SERVES 10

2 large sheets Lebanese flatbread
3 rounded tblsp hummous
½ small red sweet pepper, cut into strips
½ small yellow sweet pepper, cut into strips
½oz/15g [¼ cup] sprouting shoots, such
   as pea or leek

Heat the oven to 350°F/180°C/Gas 4.
Sprinkle the bread lightly with water and
warm it in the oven for 1-2 minutes, but
do not let it crisp. Leave it to cool and cut
into 5in/13cm x 4in/10cm oblongs.
Spread each strip of flatbread with
hummous, leaving a border around the
edges, and then divide the peppers and
sprouting shoots between them.
Fold in the bottom end and roll up, letting
the vegetables poke out at the top. Serve.

Advance preparation: cut the peppers
4 hours ahead, cover and chill. Wrap the
bread 2 hours before, cover and chill.
Freezing: not suitable.

Lettuce-wrapped Moroccan meatballs

*The aromatic Moroccan spice mixture, ras
el hanout, used in these little meatballs is
typically made with allspice, cinnamon,
cloves, coriander and cumin seeds, ginger
and peppercorns. Pork can be used instead
of lamb, although it's not a meat normally
eaten in Morocco.* SERVES 10

1 rounded tsp cornflour [cornstarch]
2 tblsp vegetable oil
10 baby cos or romaine lettuce leaves
5 mint leaves
5 coriander [cilantro] leaves
4floz/120ml chilli sauce
for the Moroccan meatballs
4oz/100g minced [ground] lamb, or pork
1 spring onion [scallion], chopped
2 tsp ras el hanout
2 tblsp chopped coriander [cilantro]
2 tblsp white sesame seeds
Salt & freshly ground black pepper

Lettuce-wrapped Moroccan meatballs

Mix all the ingredients together for the
meatballs and roll into 20 balls.
Sprinkle the cornflour on a tray and roll
the balls in it to lightly coat.
Heat the oil in a frying pan and fry the
meatballs in batches over a medium heat
for 3-4 minutes until well browned.
Remove with a slotted spoon to drain on
paper towels. Let them cool a little.
Put a warm meatball on each lettuce leaf
and place a mint or coriander leaf on top.
Serve with the chilli sauce to dip.

Advance preparation: fry the meatballs
8 hours before, cool, cover and chill.
Reheat them at 375°F/190°C/Gas 5 for
10 minutes until hot. Prepare the lettuce,
coriander and mint, cover and chill up to
8 hours before.
*Freezing: the meatballs can be frozen
cooked or uncooked 4 weeks ahead.*

Shiitake mushroom & ginger chopsticks

*The mushroom filling in this recipe also
makes a good ravioli stuffing.* SERVES 10

1 tblsp cornflour [cornstarch]
20 won-ton wrappers
Vegetable oil, for deep-frying
Chinese plum sauce, to dip
for the shiitake mushroom & ginger filling
6 tblsp toasted sesame oil
2oz/50g [6 tblsp] shallots, finely chopped
8oz/225g fresh shiitake mushrooms,
   roughly chopped

1 clove garlic, crushed
2 tsp finely grated ginger
1 tsp five-spice powder
Salt & freshly ground black pepper

Heat the sesame oil in a pan over a
medium heat, add the shallots and fry for
2-3 minutes. Stir in the mushrooms,
garlic and ginger and cook for 6 minutes
until softened. Season with five-spice
powder, salt and pepper. Set aside to cool.
Dust a work surface lightly with cornflour
and separate the won-ton wrappers.
Brush a ½in/1cm strip of water along one
side of a won-ton wrapper. Lay another
on top of this dampened edge, giving one
long wrapper. Press together to seal, then
repeat with the remaining wrappers.
Spoon some of the mushroom mixture
down one of the long sides of each
extended won-ton wrapper, leaving a
½in/1cm gap at both ends.
Brush the opposite side and the ends
lightly with water and then roll each
wrapper away from you to make a long
chopstick-like roll. Pinch the ends to seal.
Heat the vegetable oil to 350°F/180°C in
a large pan or deep-fryer. Fry the rolls in
batches for 2-3 minutes until crisp and
golden. Drain on paper towels and cool.
Serve with the plum sauce to dip.

Advance preparation: fry the rolls up to
6 hours in advance and store chilled on a
tray lined with paper towels and covered
with paper. Reheat at 400°F/200°C/Gas 6
for 5-7 minutes. Alternatively, place on a

tray dusted with cornflour, cover and chill for 4 hours before frying to order.
Freezing: freeze the mushroom mixture up to 4 weeks ahead.

Crispy duck pancakes

You can either serve this dish so that guests assemble their own, or wrapped and ready-to-go as in this recipe. MAKES 10

1 tsp salt
3 x 8oz/225g duck breasts
1 tsp five-spice powder
5 tblsp hoisin sauce
10 Chinese pancakes
5 spring onions [scallions], sliced
  diagonally
½ cucumber, seeded & cut into thin strips
1oz/25g [¼ cup] beansprouts
10 chives

Salt the skin side of the duck breasts and leave for 8 hours uncovered in the fridge to draw out the moisture. Wipe dry and rub in the five-spice powder.

Heat the oven to 400°F/200°C/Gas 6. Dry-fry the duck breasts in a frying pan over a medium high heat, skin side down, for 5 minutes.

Transfer the duck to a roasting pan and cook in the oven for 10 minutes, skin-side uppermost, until the skin is brown and crisp and the flesh is medium rare. Allow an extra 10 minutes for well done. Remove from the oven and cool.

Split each duck breast in half, then cut them crossways into thin strips. Toss the duck in the hoisin sauce.

Divide the duck, spring onions, cucumber and beansprouts between the pancakes. Roll up and tie a chive around the middle, securing with a knot. Serve.

Advance preparation: cook the duck, prepare the spring onions and cucumber 8 hours ahead, cover and chill. Assemble 1 hour before serving.
Freezing: not suitable.

right Crispy duck pancakes

Radishes with watercress butter

Any spare watercress butter can be used for filling tiny baked potatoes, in sandwiches (the pepperiness helps the flavour of cucumber no end) or piped onto Parmesan Toasts (page 54). MAKES 20

10 radishes, halved lengthways
for the watercress butter
2oz/50g [4 tblsp] unsalted butter, softened
1oz/25g watercress leaves
1 small clove garlic, crushed
Salt & freshly ground black pepper
You will also need a piping bag and small plain nozzle

Blend all the ingredients for the watercress butter in a food processor until fairly smooth. Adjust the seasoning to taste.
Trim a thin slice from the base of each halved radish to stop them toppling over. Pipe or spoon the butter on top. Serve.

Radishes with watercress butter

Advance preparation: the radishes can be topped 4 hours in advance, covered and chilled. Remove from the fridge 30 minutes before serving.
Freezing: the watercress butter can be frozen up to 4 weeks ahead.

Celery with olive & parsley salad

Gay Bilson's recipe from Stephanie Alexander's book Stephanie's Australia *was the source of the salad, which I have changed a little. She serves it as a first course with parmesan shavings and some deep-fried water crackers. Over the years I have found myriad uses for it and often make a chunky version with anchovies and sun-dried tomatoes to scatter over sliced mozzarella (page 129).* MAKES 10

2 large stalks celery, cut diagonally into 5
for the olive & parsley salad
1oz/25g [3 tblsp] pitted black olives, chopped
1 rounded tblsp diced red onion
1 rounded tblsp chopped parsley
½oz/15g [1 tblsp] capers
2 tsp olive oil
1 small clove garlic, crushed
Freshly ground black pepper
A few curls of lemon zest, to garnish

Toss all the ingredients together for the olive-parsley salad, except the lemon zest.
Spoon the salad into the celery lengths and garnish with the curls of zest.

Advance preparation: crush the garlic, chop the olives, onion and parsley and store separately, covered in the fridge, up to 1 day before. Combine the salad and fill the celery up to 4 hours ahead.
Freezing: not suitable.

Chicory with roquefort, pecans & cranberries

These ingredients also make a good autumnal fork salad if you toss them in a walnut oil dressing. SERVES 10

1 head chicory [Belgian endive]
½oz/15g [1½ tblsp] dried cranberries
¾oz/20g [2 tblsp] pecans or walnuts, roughly chopped
1½oz/40g [⅓ cup] roquefort, crumbled
A few sprigs of watercress

Trim the base of the chicory using a diagonal cut then separate the leaves.

Toss the cranberries, nuts and roquefort together in a bowl, being careful not to break up the roquefort too much.
Spoon the mixture into the chicory leaves and garnish with the watercress.

Advance preparation: fill the chicory leaves up to 3 hours before, cover and chill. Garnish just before serving.
Freezing: not suitable.

Prawn & cucumber hearts with sweet chilli sauce

Slices of cucumber make neat containers for strongly flavoured fillings, like Szechwan Chicken (page 59), Olive & Parsley Salad (left), lemony crab (page 33) and crispy vegetables (page 33). For weddings, a pretty and romantic touch is to stamp the cucumber into hearts. MAKES 10

1 large cucumber [English cucumber]
1 spring onion [scallion]
20 small peeled cooked prawns or shrimps
2 tsp sweet chilli sauce
A few curls of lemon zest
You will also need a 1½in/4cm heart-shaped or round cutter

Cut the cucumber into 10 diagonal slices ½in/1cm thick so they are wide enough to fit the cutter. Stamp out shapes using the cutter, which will also remove the skin.
Place the cucumber on a plate lined with paper towels and lay some more paper on top to absorb the excess moisture. Leave for about 1 hour to dry.
Slice the spring onion into 1¼in/3cm lengths and then again into long, fine strips. Put into a bowl of iced water for 1 hour so that the strips become curly. Dry on paper towels.
Arrange 2 prawns on each cucumber heart, spoon over some chilli sauce and garnish with the spring onion and zest.

Advance preparation: 12 hours before, stamp the cucumber and lay on paper; put the spring onion strips in water. Cover both and chill. Fill 2 hours before.
Freezing: not suitable.

Pesto, tapenade & sun-dried tomato potatoes

Bite-sized or man-sized, Mediterranean potatoes are always a hit, whether they are for drinks or supper parties. To make smooth versions of the pesto and tapenade, blend them thoroughly in a food processor or grind using a pestle and mortar. MAKES 30

30 x 1½oz/40g potatoes
½oz/15g [2 tblsp] parmesan, grated
Salt & freshly ground black pepper
for the sun-dried tomato paste
1oz/25g [3 tblsp] sun-dried tomatoes in
   oil, roughly chopped
½ tblsp sun-dried tomato oil, reserved
   from the tomatoes, or olive oil
½oz/15g [2 tblsp] parmesan, grated
for the chunky pesto
(makes 3oz/75g/¼ cup)
1oz/25g [½ cup] basil, or coriander
   [cilantro] leaves
1oz/25g [2½ tblsp] pinenuts, toasted
1 small clove garlic, crushed
1 tblsp olive oil
1oz/25g [¼ cup] parmesan, grated
Salt & freshly ground black pepper
for the chunky tapenade
(makes 3oz/75g/¼ cup)
1½oz/40g [¼ cup] pitted black olives
2 rounded tblsp parsley leaves
¾oz/20g [2 tblsp] capers
1 tsp Dijon mustard
1 tblsp olive oil
Freshly ground black pepper

Mix together all the ingredients for the sun-dried tomato paste.
Make the chunky pesto by chopping the basil or coriander roughly and placing it in a bowl with the pinenuts, garlic, olive oil, parmesan and seasoning. Mix well.
Make the chunky tapenade by roughly chopping the olives, parsley and capers together. Place them in a bowl with the mustard, olive oil and seasoning and stir.
Boil the potatoes for 5-8 minutes until tender. Cut a lid from each and discard.
Hollow out the potatoes with a teaspoon and mash the flesh with a fork. Divide the flesh between 3 bowls.
Add the sun-dried tomato paste to one batch, the pesto to another and the

Celery with olive & parsley salad

tapenade to the third. Mix each batch well with some seasoning.
Heat the oven to 375°F/190°C/Gas 5. Separately fill the potato shells with the flavoured mixtures, sprinkle with parmesan and bake them for 10 minutes until golden brown and piping hot. Serve.

Advance preparation: make the sun-dried tomato paste and tapenade up to 4 days before, cover and chill. Normally, you would make a chunky pesto at the last minute as the basil will discolour if stored. However, since the basil will lose some of its colour on baking, it is fine to make it up to 1 day before. If you are making a smooth pesto, it can be blended up to 4 days ahead and stored covered with a film of olive oil; pour off the oil before using. You can also cook and fill the potatoes up to 1 day ahead, then cover and chill. Reheat them for 15 minutes at 375°F/190°C/Gas 5.
Freezing: not suitable.

Above: *the basic cheddar cracker recipe can be used in many ways. Here it is topped with soft goat cheese, sliced tomatoes and purple basil.* Right: *as an alternative to traditional marzipan fruit cake, a delicious heart-shaped chocolate sachertorte topped with rosepetals is a stunning choice and can double as dessert. Bake it in large or small cake pans and choose the petals to match the bouquet and decorations.*

the menu

Herbed brioche sandwiches

Prawn & cucumber hearts with sweet chilli sauce

Cheddar crackers with goat cheese, tomatoes & basil

Parmesan, rocket & salsa verde sandwiches

Elderflower jellies

Summer berry tartlets

Vanilla shortbreads with fromage frais & lime curd

Heart cake with rosepetals

Jasmine infusion

wedding

Above: *it is a special occasion, so offer a welcoming non-alcoholic drink such as the Jasmine Infusion in the prettiest glasses you can find and serve them from a matching tray. Sugar swizzle sticks allow guests to sweeten the drinks to their taste and add a sense of fun.* **Right:** *choose a variety of tiny perfect fruits for the tartlets and display them in rows of uniform colour for maximum impact.*

Left: *these pretty sandwiches are also easy to make. Rounds of brioche are dipped in lemony mayonnaise then rolled in herbs. Serve with Parmesan, Rocket and Salsa Verde Sandwiches cut into squares.* Below: *a choice of dessert canapés presented on platters chosen to suit the occasion – at a wedding, it is important that the serving dishes, glasses and table decorations reflect the couple's sense of style.*

Left: *a heart-shaped cutter is all
that is needed to turn slices of
cucumber into a romantic party
piece. Here the cucumber base is
topped with fresh prawns or shrimp
and sweet chilli sauce – there is no
reason why wedding food should
not have a contemporary flavour.*
Above: *light and cool, fruit jellies
made from elderflower cordial and
a variety of fresh berries appeal to
guests of all ages.*

Hot dogs

For an Americana party, serve these hot dogs with mini hamburgers (right), Maryland crab cakes (page 51) and tiny Thanksgiving croustades (page 51). MAKES 10

1 small onion, finely sliced
1oz/25g [2 tblsp] butter
1 tblsp vegetable oil
10 mini hot dog rolls [buns]
5 mini frankfurters, halved lengthways
1 tblsp tomato ketchup
1 tblsp American mustard
Salt & freshly ground black pepper
You will also need 2 piping bags and
2 x ¼in/5mm plain nozzles

Fry the onion in the butter and oil over a low heat for about 20-30 minutes, stirring often, until soft and rich golden. Season.
Heat the oven to 375°F/190°C/Gas 5. Split the hot dog rolls and fill each with some of the onions and a frankfurter half. Transfer to a baking sheet and bake for 6-8 minutes until hot.
Spoon the ketchup and the mustard separately into piping bags fitted with nozzles and pipe a decorative squiggle of each onto the frankfurters. Serve.

Advance preparation: cook the onions up to 2 days ahead, cover and chill. Fill the hot dog rolls with the onions and frankfurters up to 3 hours before, cover and chill. Bake to order.
Freezing: the onions can be cooked and frozen up to 4 weeks before.

Hamburgers

Hamburgers

In this recipe, the Maryland crab cakes (page 51) can be substituted for the hamburger mixture if you prefer. The chilli relish will taste great with both. MAKES 10

Vegetable oil, for frying
10 mini hamburger rolls [buns],
  split in half
5 tsp chilli relish
A few leaves of curly endive
for the hamburgers
7oz/200g minced [ground] beef
2oz/50g [½ cup] shallots, finely chopped
2 tblsp Worcestershire sauce
1 tblsp tomato ketchup
Salt & freshly ground black pepper

Mix all the ingredients together for the burgers. Divide the mixture into 10 balls, flatten and shape into burgers.
Fry in batches in hot oil for 2-3 minutes on either side until cooked through.
Spread the base of the rolls with the relish, top with a few leaves of curly endive, then the burgers. Put the lids on top and serve.

Advance preparation: mix and shape the burgers, chill and cover up to 3 hours ahead. Fry and fill to order.
Freezing: not suitable.

Cheddar scones with mustard butter & ham

These cheddar scones are the best ever! Boastful, I know, but true. As with all scone mixtures, try to handle the dough as little as possible for a light result. If you are able, bake and serve them straight from the oven, filled or unfilled. MAKES 10

1oz/25g [2 tblsp] unsalted butter,
  softened
1 rounded tsp grain mustard
2½oz/60g wafer-thin ham, cut into 10
Salt & freshly ground black pepper
for the cheddar scones
5oz/150g plain flour [1 cup all-purpose
  flour], sifted + extra for rolling
1 slightly rounded tsp baking powder
½ tsp sugar

A large pinch of salt

5floz/150ml double cream [heavy cream]

4 tblsp milk

1½oz/40g [heaped ⅓ cup] mature cheddar, grated

½oz/15g [1 tblsp] melted unsalted butter + extra for greasing

You will also need a 1½in/4cm round cutter

Mix the flour, baking powder, sugar and salt together in a bowl. Add the cream, milk and 1oz/25g [¼ cup] of the cheese and gently mix together just enough to combine into a soft dough.

Turn out the dough onto a floured surface and knead very lightly, just once or twice, to incorporate the cream and cheese.

Roll the dough out gently to a thickness of ½in/1cm and stamp out the scones. Reroll and stamp out any trimmings, remembering they will not be as light as the first batch, nor will they rise as evenly.

Heat the oven to 400°F/200°C/Gas 6. Transfer the scones to a greased baking tray and set aside for 10 minutes to rest.

Brush the tops of the scones with the melted butter and sprinkle with the remaining cheese.

Bake the scones for about 10 minutes in the hot oven until well risen and golden.

Remove to a wire rack to cool if filling, otherwise, serve straight from the oven.

Mix the softened butter, mustard and seasoning together and divide the mixture between the split scones. Add a piece of ham to each scone and serve.

Advance preparation: bake the scones up to 8 hours before and store in an air-tight container. Fill 1 hour before serving, cover and keep cool.

Freezing: freeze the unbaked scones up to 2 weeks before; bake straight from the freezer in hot oven at 375°F/190°C/Gas 5 for 15 minutes. Baked scones can be frozen up to 3 weeks ahead and reheated at 350°F/180°C/Gas 4 .

left Hot dogs

Bacon & egg croustades

These miniature versions of a traditional cooked breakfast are a fiddle to make, but they never fail to please and amuse guests. I often serve them to kick off brunches, or to end late-night drinks parties. MAKES 12

4 thin slices white bread, crusts removed
1oz/25g [2 tblsp] butter, melted + extra
  for greasing
2 slices rindless streaky bacon [2 thick
  slices bacon]
12 small wild mushrooms, or 3 small
  button mushrooms, quartered
½oz/15g [1 tblsp] butter
12 quail eggs
3 very small cherry tomatoes, quartered
Salt & freshly ground black pepper
*You will also need a set of 12 round
tartlet tins 1½in/4cm in diameter*

Heat the oven to 375°F/190°C/Gas 5.
Roll the bread out thinly with a rolling pin
and cut each slice into 4 quarters.
Grease the tartlet tins and line them with
the bread, pressing it down into the
bottom and up the sides of the tin, to
make a four-cornered case.
Brush the cases well with the melted
butter and bake for 7-10 minutes until
golden brown. Remove from the tins to
a baking sheet (if making the canapés
all at once, leave the oven on).
Grill [broil] or pan-fry the bacon for
2-3 minutes until crisp. Drain on paper
towels, then cut into 12 pieces.
Sauté the mushrooms in the butter over a
medium heat for 3-4 minutes until cooked.
Season and drain on paper towels.
Crack open the quail eggs and carefully
slip 1 into each of the croustades. Divide
the bacon, mushrooms and cherry
tomatoes between them and season.
Bake for 5-7 minutes until the whites of
the quail eggs are set and the rest of the
ingredients are piping hot. Serve.

Advance preparation: fill the croustades
up to 2 hours before, cover and chill.
Bake to order.
*Freezing: the cooked croustades, bacon
and mushrooms can be frozen up to
4 weeks ahead.*

Sausage & mash croustades

If you are ever making mashed potatoes for another recipe, save some and freeze it for use in this as it's such a tiny amount to have to make otherwise. You could also use my parsley mash recipe (page 36). MAKES 12

4oz/110g boiling potato, quartered
1oz/25g [2 tblsp] butter
3 chipolata sausages
Vegetable oil, for roasting
2 shallots, sliced into rings
12 croustades (see Bacon & Egg
  Croustades Recipe, left)
2 tsp tomato ketchup

Cook the potato in a pan of salted water
for 15-20 minutes or until tender. Drain
and purée whilst still hot, using a mouli-
legumes, ricer or a sieve (using a food
processor will make the potato gluey).
Add half the butter, season and mix well.
Heat the oven to 375°F/190°C/Gas 5.
Cook the sausages with a little oil in the
oven for 10-15 minutes until golden
brown. Drain on paper towels and slice
each sausage diagonally into 8.
Fry the shallots in the remaining butter
over a medium heat for 5 minutes or until
crisp and golden. Drain on paper towels.
Fill each of the croustades with some
potato purée, 2 slices of sausage and a
few shallot rings.
Warm the croustades through in the hot
oven for 5-8 minutes. Spoon on some
ketchup before serving.

Advance preparation: fill the croustades
up to 2 hours before, cover and chill.
Bake to order.
*Freezing: the cooked croustades, mashed
potato and shallots can be frozen up to
4 weeks before.*

Miniature British Christmas dinners

Although everyone loves these Lilliputian Christmas dinners in a bite, they do take time to make. The bread sauce is a cheat's version that I have developed for speed since it is such a tiny amount to prepare. But if you want to make the real thing, do so. MAKES 12

3 button Brussels sprouts
1½ tblsp breadcrumbs
1½ tblsp creamy milk
A small pinch of nutmeg
A small piece of butter
1 slice rindless streaky bacon [1 thick
  slice bacon]
12 croustades (see Bacon & Egg
  Croustades Recipe, left)
3oz/75g cooked turkey breast, cut into 12
A few crisps [potato chips], broken into 24
3 tblsp chicken or turkey gravy
Salt & freshly ground black pepper

Boil the Brussels sprouts in a pan of
salted water for 7-8 minutes, or until
tender. Drain, refresh in cold water, dry
on paper towels and then cut each sprout
into 4 even pieces.
Make the bread sauce by soaking the
crumbs in the milk for 5 minutes. Warm
through over a low heat for 2-3 minutes.
Add the nutmeg, seasoning and the butter
to make a spoonable consistency. Stir well
and remove from the heat to cool.
Cook the bacon under the grill [broiler],
or pan-fry, for 2-3 minutes until crisp.
Drain on paper towels and then cut the
bacon into 12 pieces. Cool.
Heat the oven to 375°F/190°C/Gas 5.
Fill the prepared croustades with a piece
of turkey, Brussels sprout, bacon and
some crisps. Spoon on the bread sauce.
Place the filled croustades on a baking
sheet and warm through in the oven for
5-8 minutes until hot. Heat the gravy
separately in a saucepan and spoon it
over the croustades before serving.

Advance preparation: fill the croustades,
except for the gravy, up to 2 hours before,
cover and chill. Bake to order.
*Freezing: the cooked croustades can be
frozen up to 4 weeks before.*

Cornmeal muffins with Maryland crab cakes

Miniature Thanksgiving dinners

Another recipe requiring nimble fingers: a bite-sized taste of Thanksgiving. MAKES 12

3oz/75g sweet potato, quartered
A small piece of butter
2 ears baby corn
12 croustades (see Bacon & Egg Croustades Recipe, left)
3oz/75g cooked turkey breast, cut into 12
3 tblsp chicken or turkey gravy
2 rounded tsp cranberry sauce
Salt & freshly ground black pepper

Cook the sweet potato in a pan of salted water for 15-20 minutes until tender. Drain, pass through a sieve, stir in the butter and seasoning and allow to cool.
Boil the baby corn in a pan of salted water for 2-3 minutes, or until tender. Drain, refresh in cold water, dry on paper towels and cut each ear into 12 rounds.
Heat the oven to 375°F/190°C/Gas 5. Fill the croustades with some sweet potato purée, a piece of turkey and 2 slices of corn, then bake for 5-8 minutes until hot.
Warm the gravy in a saucepan and divide it between the filled croustades. Top with the cranberry sauce just before serving.

Advance preparation: fill the croustades, except for the gravy, up to 2 hours before, cover and chill. Bake to order.
Freezing: the cooked croustades and the sweet potato purée can be frozen up to 4 weeks before.

Cornmeal muffins with Maryland crab cakes

These buttery yellow cornmeal muffins, flecked with chilli and coriander, can be served unfilled straight from the oven if you like. Tapenade and chunky guacamole are good alternative fillings. MAKES 12

Vegetable oil, for frying
Salt & freshly ground black pepper
12 coriander [cilantro] leaves

for the cornmeal muffins
2oz/50g plain flour [½ cup all-purpose flour]
2oz/50g [6½ tblsp] yellow cornmeal
1 tsp baking powder
A pinch of salt
1oz/25g [2 tblsp] butter, melted + extra for greasing
1 small egg, lightly beaten
3 tblsp milk
1 tsp finely chopped red bird's-eye chilli
1 tblsp chopped coriander [cilantro]
for the Maryland crab cakes
2½oz/60g [½ cup] cooked white crab meat
3 tblsp white breadcrumbs
1 tsp finely chopped red bird's-eye chilli
1 tblsp chopped coriander [cilantro]
3 tblsp mayonnaise
1 small egg, lightly beaten
You will also need a set of 12 round mini muffin tins 1½in/4cm in diameter

Heat the oven to 350°F/180°C/Gas 4. Prepare the muffins by sifting the flour, cornmeal, baking powder and salt together into a bowl. Make a well in the centre and quickly stir in the butter, egg, milk, chilli and coriander. Mix well.
Grease the muffin tins and then divide the muffin mixture between them.
Bake the muffins for 10-12 minutes, or until risen and golden. Remove to a wire rack to cool and then split in half.
Mix all the ingredients for the crab cakes together and season well. Divide the mixture into 12 balls, then flatten and shape them into little cakes.
Fry the crab cakes in batches in hot oil for 1 minute on either side until cooked. Remove them from the heat and quickly drain on paper towels.
Fill each of the muffins with a hot crab cake and a coriander leaf and serve.

Advance preparation: make the muffins up to 8 hours before and store in an airtight container. Mix and shape the crab cakes, chill and cover up to 4 hours ahead. Fry and fill to order.
Freezing: make the muffins and freeze up to 3 weeks before. Warm the muffins in a preheated oven at 350°F/180°C/Gas 4 for 3-4 minutes to freshen, then cool.

Brioche filled with wild mushrooms or scrambled eggs & caviar

If your budget does not stretch to caviar, as in this recipe, use some finely chopped smoked salmon and snipped chives with the eggs instead. A small nugget of foie gras slipped into the hollowed-out brioche and warmed through also makes a sublime, albeit pricey, filling but chopped smoked ham and sautéed leeks stirred in a thick cheesy sauce is equally good. MAKES 20

20 bite-sized brioche or savoury muffins
for the wild mushroom filling
5oz/150g small wild mushooms
½oz/15g [1 tblsp] unsalted butter
1 tblsp olive oil
½ small clove garlic, crushed
A large pinch of fresh thyme leaves
Salt & freshly ground black pepper
for the scrambled eggs & caviar filling
2 medium eggs, lightly beaten
½oz/15g [1 tblsp] unsalted butter
1 tblsp double cream [heavy cream]
2oz/50g sevruga caviar
Salt & freshly ground black pepper

Cut the tops off the brioche, reserving the lids. Hollow out the brioche using a small sharp knife or melon baller.
Sauté the mushrooms in the butter, olive oil and garlic over a medium heat until cooked, about 3-4 minutes. Stir in the thyme and seasoning and leave to cool.
Spoon the mushroom mixture into 10 of the brioche and put the lids on top.
Heat the oven to 350°F/180°C/Gas 4. Put the filled and the unfilled brioche separately on baking trays and cover loosely with foil. Warm the filled brioche in the oven for 10-12 minutes and the unfilled brioche for 2-3 minutes only.
Pass the eggs through a sieve. Melt the butter in a small heavy pan over a very low heat, add the eggs and stir constantly for 2-3 minutes, until the eggs are creamy and just hold their shape.
Remove from the heat. Stir in the cream, season, then transfer the eggs to a bowl.

left Saffron mussels in garlic bread

Spoon the eggs into the warm brioche, top with the caviar and the lids and serve alongside the mushroom brioche.

Advance preparation: up to 4 hours before, hollow out all the brioche, cover and put 10 of them aside. Fill the rest with the cold sautéed mushrooms, cover and chill. Warm the filled brioche in an oven set to 350°F/180°C/Gas 4 for 5-7 minutes. Fill the others to order.
Freezing: not suitable.

Camembert ice-cream on parmesan toasts

Camembert ice-cream, accompanied by the parmesan toasts, is an unusual canapé but also makes a fabulous cheese course at lunch or supper. My basic recipe is taken from Jane Grigson's book Good Things. *She liked to serve it with heated water biscuits, and quite delicious it is too. MAKES 10*

½ x Parmesan Toasts Recipe (page 54)
A few small salad leaves, such as rocket
 [arugula] or mustard greens
for the camembert ice-cream
4oz/110g ripe camembert or brie, peeled
4 tblsp single cream [light cream]
4 tblsp double cream [heavy cream]
Tabasco sauce, or cayenne pepper
Salt

Blend the cheese and single cream together in a food processor for about 30 seconds or until smooth. Stir in the double cream and season well with Tabasco or cayenne and salt.
Transfer the mixture to a lidded plastic container and freeze for about 3-4 hours or until firm (there is no need to stir it).
Unmould the ice-cream onto a board, cut off small shavings with a sharp knife and arrange on the parmesan toasts.
Garnish each of the canapés with a single salad leaf and serve.

Advance preparation: top the parmesan toasts with the ice-cream just 5 minutes before serving.
Freezing: make and freeze the ice-cream up to 2 weeks in advance.

Saffron mussels in garlic bread

Garlic, saffron and mussels: a marriage made in heaven. MAKES 10

10 x 1in/2.5cm slices small baguette
1 medium clove garlic
for the saffron mussels
2 shallots, finely chopped
1 small clove garlic, crushed
1oz/25g [2 tblsp] butter
4 tblsp white wine
7oz/200g small fresh mussels
5floz/150ml double cream [heavy cream]
5-6 saffron threads
1 tblsp chopped parsley
Salt & freshly ground black pepper

Heat the oven to 375°F/190°C/Gas 5. Scoop some of the bread out of the centre of the baguette slices. Rub the bread all over with the garlic. Bake for 5-8 minutes until just coloured and slightly crisp.
Cook the shallots in the butter in a large pan over a medium heat for 5 minutes until softened.
Pour in the wine, increase the heat to high, stir well and then add the mussels. Cover and steam for 4-5 minutes until all the shells have opened. Discard any that remain unopened.
Lift out the mussels with a slotted spoon and cool before removing the meat from the shells. Strain and reserve the liquid.
Set the oven to 350°F/180°C/Gas 4. Put the baguette slices into the oven to warm through for 1-2 minutes.
Stir the cream, saffron and parsley into the mussel juices and, if necessary, reduce the liquid by boiling down to a coating consistency. Season to taste.
Return the mussel meat to the pan and heat through for 1-2 minutes over a medium heat. Spoon the mussels and sauce onto the warm bread and serve.

Advance preparation: combine the mussels and sauce 6 hours before, cover and chill. Warm for 4-5 minutes over a moderate heat until very hot. Fill the warmed baguette slices to order.
Freezing: the baked baguette slices can be frozen up to 4 weeks ahead.

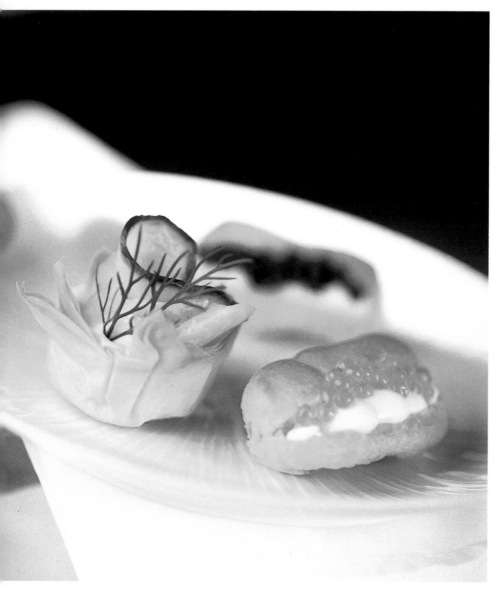

left to right Smoked trout & cucumber filo tartlets, Caviar éclairs

Heat the oven to 375°F/190°C/Gas 5. Bake the straws for 8-10 minutes until golden brown. Transfer to a wire rack to cool. Serve warm or cold.

Advance preparation: bake the straws 4 days before and store in an airtight container. Warm through in a preheated oven set to 350°F/180°C/Gas 4 for 3-4 minutes to crisp up.
Freezing: freeze the straws unbaked up to 4 weeks before and bake from frozen, or freeze them baked 3 weeks ahead and warm through as above.

Parmesan toasts

These cheesy toasts are an updated version of melba toast and a good way to use up any bread that is past its best. Serve them at drinks parties when you want something very plain amongst more complicated canapés, or top with Camembert Ice-cream (page 53). At stand-up fork buffets, parmesan toasts are an extremely practical bread to serve as they do not require any butter and therefore no unnecessary knives either. MAKES 20

20 very thin slices bread, such as
   ciabatta, focaccia or baguette
2oz/50g [4 tblsp] butter, melted, or
   olive oil
3 tblsp finely grated parmesan
Salt & freshly ground black pepper

Heat the oven to 375°F/190°C/Gas 5. Divide the sliced bread between some baking trays and brush the upper sides of the bread with the melted butter. Liberally sprinkle with the parmesan and season well with salt and pepper.
Bake the toasts on two shelves in the oven for 8-12 minutes or until crisp and golden, swapping the trays over halfway through cooking. Cool before serving.

Advance preparation: make the toasts up to 1 week in advance and store in an airtight container. Warm through in a preheated oven at 350°F/180°C/Gas 4 for 2-3 minutes to crisp up.
Freezing: make and freeze up to 4 weeks ahead. Warm through as above.

Sesame cheese straws

When friends are coming over for a quick drink, I like to serve these with a mixture of other simple nibbles, such as parmesan toasts and anchovy pastries. They can all be pulled out of the freezer and quickly warmed through to freshen them up. MAKES 30

3½oz/95g [7 tblsp] unsalted butter +
   extra for greasing
4½oz/125g plain flour [scant 1 cup all-
   purpose flour] + extra for rolling
4oz/110g [1 cup] mature cheddar,
   coarsely grated
½ tsp cayenne pepper
A large pinch of salt
2 tsp sesame seeds
You will also need a fluted pasta wheel

Mix the butter and flour together in a food processor for 30 seconds or until they resemble fine breadcrumbs. Add the cheese, cayenne and salt and pulse 4-5 times, just until a dough forms.
Transfer to a lightly floured surface and knead the pastry for 1 minute. Wrap in plastic wrap and chill for 30 minutes.
Roll out the dough to a thickness of ¼in/4mm on a lightly floured surface and then, using a fluted pasta wheel, cut the pastry into straws about 6in/14cm long x ½in/1.5cm wide. Re-roll the trimmings to the same thickness and cut to make a total of 30 straws.
Sprinkle the pastries with sesame seeds, then lift them onto lightly greased baking trays. Chill for 30 minutes.

Anchovy pastries

If, like me, you love salty foods, anchovy pastries fit the bill nicely. MAKES 10

5oz/150g puff pastry
Flour, for rolling
5 salted anchovies, rinsed & drained
1 tsp butter, melted

Roll out the pastry very thinly on a lightly floured surface to a square measuring 8in/20cm. Cut the pastry square in half.
Lay the anchovies, one beneath the other, across the width of one piece of pastry, leaving a gap between each anchovy.
Brush the remaining piece of pastry with water, turn it over and lift it onto the anchovy-topped pastry. Press down firmly between each anchovy and brush all over with melted butter.
Cut down the length of the pastry, through the anchovies, to give 10 equal strips. Transfer the pastries to a lightly greased baking tray and chill for 30 minutes.
Heat the oven to 375°F/190°C/Gas 5. Bake the pastries for 8 minutes or until golden. Serve warm or cold.

Advance preparation: bake up to 1 day before, store in an airtight box and reheat in the oven at 350°F/180°C/Gas 4 for 2-3 minutes to crisp up.
Freezing: freeze the pastries 3 weeks before and warm through as above.

Curry puffs

These Indian-style puff pastries are best served straight from the oven as they become too dry if reheated. MAKES 10

4½oz/125g puff pastry
4 tsp medium-hot curry paste
Butter, for greasing
1 small egg yolk
1 tsp water
½ tsp salt
½ tsp cumin seeds
Flour, for rolling
You will also need a 2in/5cm fluted cutter

Roll the pastry out on a lightly floured surface to a thickness of ⅛in/2mm and trim to give an oblong of pastry measuring 8in/20cm x 10in/25cm. Cut the pastry into 3 oblongs 8in/20cm x 3¼in/8cm.
Divide the curry paste between 2 of the oblongs, spread the mixture to the edges and stack the sheets on top of each other. Put the last oblong on top and roll lightly to give a stack ¼in/5mm thick.
Stamp out 10 discs using the cutter. Lift them onto a lightly greased baking tray, leaving a little space between each.
Mix the egg yolk, water and salt together. Brush this over the tops of the pastries and sprinkle with the cumin. Do not let the egg drip over the sides as this will stop the pastry rising. Chill for 30 minutes.
Heat the oven to 375°F/190°C/Gas 5 and bake the puffs for 8-10 minutes until they are well risen and golden. Serve hot.

Advance preparation: make up to the stage of glazing, cover and chill up to 1 day ahead. Glaze and bake as above.
Freezing: freeze uncooked up to 4 weeks before. Bake as above.

Caviar éclairs

Who wants a chocolate éclair when you can have a caviar-filled éclair instead? Lumpfish roe is no substitute for real caviar so do not even think about using it! MAKES 16

1 x Choux Pastry Recipe (page 81)
Butter, for greasing
6 tblsp crème fraîche
1½oz/40g sevruga caviar
1½oz/40g salmon caviar
You will also need a piping bag and plain ½in/1cm nozzle.

Heat the oven to 400°F/200°C/Gas 6. Put the pastry into a piping bag and pipe 2in/5cm lengths of the pastry, well apart, on a lightly greased baking sheet.
Bake the éclairs for 10-12 minutes until golden. Make a slit in the side of each, return to the oven and leave the door ajar for 5 minutes to dry out the pastry.
Cool the éclairs on a wire rack and then make a bigger slit in the sides.
Spoon the crème fraîche into a piping bag fitted with a nozzle and fill the éclairs.

Garnish half with the sevruga caviar and the rest with the salmon caviar. Serve.

Advance preparation: make the éclairs up to 1 day in advance and store in an airtight container. Crisp them up for 2-3 minutes in a preheated oven at 350°F/180°C/Gas 4 and cool before filling. Fill up to 1 hour before serving.
Freezing: freeze the baked pastries up to 3 weeks ahead, crisp up and fill as above.

Smoked trout & cucumber filo tartlets

Smoked eel, mackerel or salmon can be used instead of trout in this recipe. MAKES 12

3 x 12in/30cm square sheets filo pastry
1oz/25g [2 tblsp] butter, melted
3 tblsp crème fraîche
1 tsp freshly creamed horseradish
4oz/110g smoked pink trout fillets, cut into 12
1in/2.5cm cucumber, halved, seeded & sliced into 12
A few sprigs of dill
Freshly ground black pepper
You will also need a set of 12 round tartlet tins 1½in/4cm in diameter

Brush 2 of the sheets of pastry with half the melted butter, lay them on top of each other and press the third unbuttered sheet on top. Cut into 12 equal squares.
Heat the oven to 375°F/190°C/Gas 5. Grease the tartlet tins and line them with the pastry, giving a four-cornered case.
Bake for 7-10 minutes until golden brown. Remove to a wire rack to cool.
Mix the crème fraîche and horseradish together with some black pepper and spoon into the tart cases. Arrange a piece of trout on top of each, then a cucumber slice and a sprig of dill. Serve.

Advance preparation: mix the crème fraîche and horseradish and slice the cucumber 4 hours before, cover and chill. Fill the tarts up to 15 minutes before.
Freezing: freeze the baked tart cases 3 weeks before. Reheat for 3-4 minutes at 350°F/180°C/Gas 4 then cool and fill.

Cheddar crackers, goat cheese, tomatoes & basil

I have a really wide range of toppings that I like to use for these versatile cheddar crackers. They include mozzarella and salsa verde (page 64), pesto or tapenade (page 43); chargrilled asparagus and roasted cherry tomatoes; cream cheese and chutney and also watercress butter (page 42). They are also terrific served plain. MAKES 12

⅓ (4oz/100g) x Sesame Cheese Straws dough (page 54), made without sesame seeds
Flour, for dusting
Butter, for greasing
2oz/50g goat cheese, softened
6 yellow or red cherry tomatoes, sliced into 4
A few purple or green basil leaves
You will also need a 1½in/4cm plain cutter, a piping bag and a small plain piping nozzle

Roll the pastry out to a thickness of ¼in/4mm on a lightly floured surface and then stamp out discs using the cutter. Re-roll any trimmings and stamp out again.
Lift the pastry discs onto lightly greased baking trays and chill for 30 minutes.
Heat the oven to 375°F/190°C/Gas 5. Bake the crackers for 8-10 minutes or until they are golden brown, then transfer them to a wire rack to cool.
Spoon the softened goat cheese into a piping bag fitted with a nozzle and pipe a little onto each cracker.
Arrange 2 slices of tomato on top of each mound of goat cheese, then garnish each cracker with a basil leaf and serve.

Advance preparation: bake the crackers up to 4 days before and store them in an airtight container. Reheat the crackers in the oven at 350°F/180°C/Gas 4 to crisp up, then allow them to cool before topping. Slice the tomatoes up to 4 hours ahead, cover and chill. Top the crackers 20 minutes before serving.
Freezing: freeze the crackers unbaked up to 4 weeks before and bake from frozen, or freeze baked up to 3 weeks ahead and warm through as above.

Red onion, goat cheese & courgette pastries

I often make larger versions of these pizza-like pastries, cutting them into 5½in/14cm rounds, to serve as a first course or lunch dish with salad. Do not hesitate to try different toppings, substituting roasted tomatoes for the courgettes and feta or mozzarella for the goat cheese. MAKES 10

5oz/150g puff pastry
Flour, for dusting
½oz/15g [1 tblsp] butter
½ tsp sugar
½ small red onion, sliced into wedges through the root
1 tsp red wine vinegar
1 very small courgette [zucchini], thinly sliced into rounds
1½oz/40g [⅓ cup] goat cheese
1 tblsp olive oil
2 tsp thyme leaves
Salt & freshly ground black pepper
You will also need some parchment paper

Roll the pastry out on a lightly floured surface to an oblong measuring 2in/5cm x 15in/37.5cm. Then cut the pastry into 10 even-sized oblongs measuring 2in/5cm x 1½in/3.75cm.
Lift the pastry oblongs onto a baking tray lined with parchment paper and chill them for 30 minutes.
Melt the butter and sugar together in a frying pan over a low heat, add the onion and cook for 5-8 minutes until softened. Add the vinegar and leave to cool.
Heat the oven to 400°F/200°C/Gas 6. Arrange the onion and courgettes on top of the pastries. Crumble the goat cheese over the top and drizzle with the oil. Scatter with the thyme and season thoroughly with salt and pepper.
Bake the pastries for 8 minutes until well risen and golden. Serve hot.

Advance preparation: assemble the pastries up to the point of baking and chill, covered, up to 6 hours in advance. Bake as above.
Freezing: freeze the pastries ready to bake. Cook from frozen, allowing about 10 minutes in the oven.

Mediterranean puffs

When time is short, this is a recipe where you can buy all the basics ready to do a quick assembly line job. Good puff pastry, pesto and tapenade are all readily available from supermarkets these days to make our lives easier in the kitchen. MAKES 30

14oz/400g puff pastry
Flour, for dusting
Butter, for greasing
1 small egg yolk
1 tsp water
½ tsp salt
2 tsp poppy seeds
2 tsp yellow mustard seeds
1 x Chunky Pesto Recipe (page 43), or 3oz/75g [⅓ cup] ready-made pesto
1 x Chunky Tapenade Recipe (page 43), or 3oz/75g [⅓ cup] ready-made tapenade
2oz/50g [⅓ cup] sun-dried tomatoes in oil, roughly chopped
3oz/75g [¾ cup] parmesan, grated
3oz/75g [¾ cup] cheddar, grated
You will also need a 2in/5cm fluted cutter

Roll the pastry out on a lightly floured surface to make an oblong measuring 12in/30cm x 14½in/36cm x ¼in/5mm.
Stamp out 30 pastry discs using the cutter. Lift them onto lightly greased baking trays, leaving space between each to allow them to rise. Do not re-roll the off-cuts as they will not rise evenly.
Mix the egg yolk, water and salt together in a small bowl then brush the tops of the pastries with this glaze. Do not let the glaze run over the sides of the pastries as this will stop them from rising.
Sprinkle the pastries with the poppy and mustard seeds and chill for 30 minutes.
Heat the oven to 375°F/190°C/Gas 5. Bake the pastries for 10-15 minutes until they are well risen and a rich golden colour. Cool on a wire rack.
Put the pesto, tapenade and sun-dried tomatoes into 3 separate bowls, divide the parmesan and cheddar between them and then separately pulse each batch in a blender until you have a thickish paste.
Split the cooked pastries in half. Spoon each of the fillings into 10 of the pastries and cover with the tops.

Mediterranean puffs

Place on baking trays and reheat the pastries at 375°F/190°C/Gas 5 for 10 minutes or until hot. Serve.

Advance preparation: stamp out the pastries, cover and refrigerate up to 1 day ahead. On the day, glaze, bake and fill up to 6 hours before. Reheat to order.
Freezing: freeze either uncooked and unfilled up to 4 weeks before, or cooked and unfilled up to 3 weeks before.

Quail egg & smoked salmon tartlets

Hollandaise sauce, eggs and smoked salmon are made for each other. This canapé combines them cleverly in a bite-sized treat suitable for sophisticated brunches or drinks parties. The versatile shortcrust recipe is used on several other occasions in this book. It will yield 1lb10oz/740g of pastry which in turn will make: 100 x 1½in/4cm mini tartlets; 18 x 4in/10cm individual shallow tarts; or 2 x 10in/25.5cm large shallow tarts. Make the full quantity of pastry and freeze it in batches for other occasions. MAKES 12

6 quail eggs
2½oz/60g smoked salmon, cut into
   12 pieces
A few sprigs of chervil
for the savoury shortcrust pastry
(makes 1lb10oz/740g)
1lb/450g plain flour [3 cups all-purpose
   flour], sifted + extra for dusting
A pinch of salt
8oz/225g [1 cup] unsalted butter, diced
1 large egg, beaten
1 tblsp cold water
for the hollandaise sauce
2½oz/60g [4½ tblsp] unsalted butter
1 medium egg yolk
1 tblsp lemon juice
Salt & freshly ground white pepper
*You will also need a set of 12 round
tartlet tins 1½in/4cm in diameter and a
2in/5cm plain cutter*

Put the flour, salt and butter together in a food processor and pulse 7-8 times until the mixture resembles fine breadcrumbs.
Turn into a bowl, add the egg and water and mix to a dough using a palette knife [metal spatula]. Knead well until smooth.

Wrap 4oz/110g [about ⅛] of the pastry in plastic wrap and chill for 30 minutes before using; freeze the remainder in batches for use in other recipes.
Roll out the chilled pastry thinly on a lightly floured surface and stamp out 12 discs with the cutter.
Line the tartlet tins, pressing the pastry down into the bottom and up the sides of the tin. Trim away any excess pastry, lightly prick the bases with a fork and chill for 30 minutes.
Heat the oven to 375°F/190°C/Gas 5. Bake the tartlets for 10 minutes until golden. Cool them for 10 minutes before removing from the tins to a baking tray.
Put the quail eggs in a pan of water, bring to the boil and cook for 3 minutes until hard. Drain and leave under running cold water until stone cold. Peel, rinse away any shell and dry on paper towels. Cut the eggs in half lengthways.
Make the hollandaise sauce by first melting the unsalted butter in a small pan over a low heat and discarding any froth from the surface of the liquid.
Whisk the egg yolk with a dash of cold water over a very low heat until thickened. Then, whisk in the melted butter, little by little, leaving behind any sediment in the base of the pan.
Stir the lemon juice and salt and pepper into the sauce and adjust the seasoning to taste. Remove the hollandaise from the heat and keep it warm by sitting the pan over another pan of warm water.
Heat the oven to 350°F/180°C/Gas 4. Fill the tartlet cases with a piece of salmon and half a quail egg. Cover loosely with foil and bake for 4-5 minutes, until warm, but not so hot that the salmon cooks.
Spoon some hollandaise sauce over each tartlet, garnish with chervil and serve.

Advance preparation: bake the tartlet cases up to 1 day before and store in an airtight container. Fill with the salmon and eggs up to 2 hours ahead, cover and chill. Bake to order then top with sauce.
Freezing: the tartlet cases can be frozen unbaked in their tins for up to 1 week and baked straight from the freezer. Freeze them baked up to 3 weeks ahead

Mixed bruschetta platter

The great thing about bruschetta is that they can be topped with virtually any type of food and they are an excellent way of using up leftovers. Bruschetta can even be sweet, made with fruit, as you will see later in the book (page 78). Serve this platter at parties where you want finger foods that are more substantial than the usual canapés. You can also choose just one of the bruschetta (this recipe gives 10 of each) to serve as part of a themed menu. Although bruschetta originated in Italy, do not feel restricted to Italian ingredients: the recipes here take inspiration from around the world. MAKES 50

50 x ½in/1cm slices coarse-textured
  bread, such as pugliese or sourdough
5 large cloves garlic
Olive oil, for drizzling
Salt & freshly ground black pepper
for the asparagus, prosciutto & parmesan
bruschetta
15 asparagus spears, trimmed to
  4in/10cm & cut lengthways in half
10 slices prosciutto di Parma
2oz/50g parmesan cheese, shaved
for the tomato, bocconcini & basil
bruschetta
10 plum or salad tomatoes, roughly
  chopped
10 bocconcini cheeses (tiny mozzarella),
  each cut into 3, or 2 buffalo mozzarella,
  each cut into 5
2 tblsp basil leaves, torn
for the sausage & mustard bruschetta
6 tblsp onion chutney, or tomato relish
10 cooked spicy pork sausages, sliced
  diagonally into 4
2 tblsp mustard
A few sprigs of flat-leaf parsley
for the Szechwan chicken bruschetta
1¼lb/570g cooked chicken, shredded
1 x Peanut Sauce Recipe (page 39)
¼ cucumber [English cucumber],
  quartered lengthways, seeded & cut
  into thin diagonal slices
2 spring onions [scallions], thinly sliced
1 large hot red chilli, thinly sliced
1 rounded tsp toasted sesame seeds

left Szechwan chicken bruschetta

for the seafood bruschetta
4 tblsp olive oil
1 tblsp lemon juice
1 small clove garlic, crushed
8oz/225g small cooked squid rings
8oz/225g cooked shelled mussels
8oz/225g cooked peeled prawns or
  shrimps
A few sprigs of dill
You will also need a piping bag and
¼in/5mm plain nozzle

Toast the bread on both sides until crisp under a grill [broiler] or on a very hot ridged cast-iron grill-pan. Rub the toasted bread with the garlic, pepper lightly and drizzle with some olive oil. Cool.
Put the asparagus on a hot, lightly oiled, ridged cast-iron grill-pan and cook for 4-5 minutes, turning occasionally. Cool.
Divide the prosciutto and asparagus between 10 of the bruschetta, and place a few parmesan shavings on top.

Pile the tomatoes and bocconcini onto 10 bruschetta and scatter over the basil.
Spread the chutney or relish onto 10 bruschetta and place the sausages on top. Put the mustard into a piping bag and pipe it over the sausages. Garnish with a sprig of parsley.
Arrange the chicken on 10 bruschetta, spoon over the peanut sauce, top with the cucumber and spring onions and scatter over the chilli and sesame seeds.
Mix the oil, lemon juice, garlic and seasoning together for the seafood bruschetta and toss the shellfish in this dressing. Spoon onto the rest of the bruschetta and garnish with a sprig of dill.
Arrange on a platter and serve.

Advance preparation: prepare the toppings 6 hours ahead, cover and chill separately. Make the bruschetta and top up to 1 hour ahead, cover and keep cool. *Freezing: not suitable.*

Mixed bruschetta platter

Smoked salmon & mascarpone crumpet pizzas

Scrambled eggs, crispy bacon and roasted tomatoes are a terrific brunch topping for toasted crumpets. You can also use crumpets for classic pizza toppings. Children, and adults, will adore them. MAKES 10

10 crumpets
6oz/175g [¾ cup] mascarpone
5oz/150g smoked salmon, cut into 10
4oz/110g salmon caviar
A few sprigs of mizuna & chervil
Freshly ground black pepper

Toast the crumpets on both sides under the grill [broiler] for about 1 minute on either side or until golden.
Spread with the mascarpone whilst still hot, then arrange the smoked salmon on top and grind over some black pepper.
Spoon on the caviar and put a few herb leaves on top. Serve hot.

Advance preparation: cut the salmon up to 4 hours before, cover and chill.
Freezing: not suitable.

Potato, garlic & rosemary pizzas

This is a great combination of ingredients: crisp pizza base and tender potato with lots of garlic and rosemary. Grilled, crumbled pancetta strewn on top of the potato tastes fantastic too. The yeastless pizza dough recipe, which is very quick to make, is taken from Lindsey Bareham's definitive book, In Praise of the Potato. *MAKES 10*

for the pizza base
8oz/225g strong plain flour [2 cups all-purpose flour] + extra for dusting
1 tsp bicarbonate of soda [baking soda]
1 tsp cream of tartar
5floz/150ml milk + 1 tblsp vinegar for souring
1 tsp salt
for the topping
1lb/450g waxy potatoes, very thinly sliced
5 tblsp olive oil
2 large cloves garlic, crushed

1½ tblsp finely chopped rosemary leaves
2½oz/60g [heaped ½ cup] parmesan, grated
Sea salt & freshly ground black pepper

Sift the flour, bicarbonate of soda, cream of tartar and salt into a bowl. Using a wooden spoon, gradually mix in the milk, which has been soured with the vinegar, to make a soft dough. Put the dough onto a floured surface, knead lightly and then divide into 10 portions.
Roll each piece of dough into a ball, flatten and then roll them into 4⅓in/11cm circles. Transfer the pizza bases to lightly floured baking trays.
Heat the oven to 400°F/200°C/Gas 6. Toss the potato slices with the oil, rosemary and garlic, then season.
Arrange the potato on the pizza bases in circles, slightly overlapping like a French apple tart. Sprinkle over the parmesan.
Bake for 8-10 minutes until the pizza bases are crisp and the potatoes are tender and golden brown. Serve hot.

Advance preparation: bake the pizzas up to 4 hours before and cover. Reheat at 375°F/190°C/Gas 5 for 4-5 minutes.
Freezing: not suitable.

Parmesan polenta pizzas

My pizzas come in lots of different guises and here is one where the base is not made of bread dough, but polenta that has been sliced, coated and fried. I always think the blandness of polenta is much improved when a generous amount of parmesan is added. The toppings here are classic pizza flavours; you could also use some sautéed wild mushrooms (page 111). MAKES 10

for the pizza bases
1¾ pints/1 litre [1 quart] water
13oz/365g [3 cups] instant polenta
4oz/110g [½ cup] butter
9oz/250g [2½ cups] parmesan, grated
for the coating
4oz/110g [scant 1 cup] instant polenta
4oz/110g [1 cup] parmesan, grated
2 medium eggs, lightly beaten
5floz/150ml vegetable oil

for the topping
1lb2oz/500g robiola cheese, or soft goat cheese, sliced into 20
8 roasted, or sun-dried, tomato halves, sliced
10 salted anchovies, cut into 3
1 rounded tblsp capers preserved in balsamic vinegar
Salt & freshly ground black pepper

Make the pizza bases by heating the water in a large pan until boiling. Stir in the polenta and cook for 2 minutes, stirring constantly, until thick.
Remove the polenta from the heat, stir in the butter, parmesan and lots of salt and pepper. Cool for 10 minutes.
Take a large piece of plastic wrap about 16in/40cm long x 12in/30cm wide. Spoon the cooked polenta down the centre, fold the plastic wrap over it and use this to help you shape the polenta into a smooth cylinder about 8in/20cm long x 4in/10cm wide. Chill for 1 hour.
Mix together the polenta and parmesan for the coating. Cut the chilled cooked polenta into 10 even discs, coat them in the beaten egg and then in the polenta-parmesan mixture.
Heat the oil in a pan and fry the polenta discs in batches, for 2-3 minutes on each side, until crisp. Drain on paper towels.
Put 2 slices of cheese on each polenta pizza and divide the tomatoes, anchovies and capers amongst them.
Grill [broil] the pizzas for 3-4 minutes or until the cheese has melted and the polenta is hot. Serve immediately.

Advance preparation: make the polenta up to 3 days before and chill. Coat and fry the bases up to 4 hours before, cool, top, cover and chill. Grill to order.
Freezing: not suitable.

right Parmesan polenta pizzas

Waffles with radish & cucumber fromage frais

Don't worry if you don't have a waffle iron as you can cook spoonfuls of the batter in a heavy frying pan instead. MAKES 10

for the waffles
2oz/50g spring onions, finely sliced
  [½ cup finely sliced scallions]
½oz/15g [1 tblsp] butter + extra for
  greasing
2½oz/60g self-raising flour [½ cup
  self-rising flour], sifted
½oz/15g [2 tblsp] parmesan, grated
1oz/25g [¼ cup] cheddar, grated
4floz/120ml milk
1 egg, lightly beaten
for the radish & cucumber fromage frais
7oz/200g [1⅓ cups] cucumber, seeded
  & roughly grated
2oz/50g [½ cup] radishes, roughly grated
4oz/110g [1 cup] fromage frais or blanc
1 rounded tblsp chopped mint + extra
  mint leaves to garnish
Salt & freshly ground black pepper

Cook the spring onions in the butter over a low heat for 2-3 minutes until soft. Transfer to a large bowl and leave to cool.
Add the flour and cheeses to the spring onions and make a well in the centre. Pour in the milk, egg and seasoning and mix well to make a thickish batter. Whisk for 30 seconds and then let the batter stand for 5 minutes before using.
Heat a waffle iron and lightly grease with butter. Pour in half the batter and cook the waffles for 2-3 minutes or until golden brown. Transfer to a wire rack to cool. Repeat with the remaining batter, then break the cooked waffles into sections. Alternatively, cook spoonfuls of the batter on a greased, heavy-based frying pan for about 2 minutes on each side.
Reserve 1 tablespoon each of the grated cucumber and radish for garnishing. Mix the rest into the fromage frais with the chopped mint and seasoning.
Divide the topping between the waffles, garnish with the reserved cucumber and radish and a sprig of mint. Serve.

left Waffles with radish & cucumber fromage frais

Advance preparation: cook the waffles 12 hours before and store in an airtight box. Refresh at 350°F/180°C/Gas 4 for 2-3 minutes and cool before using. Make the fromage frais topping 1 hour before and top the waffles 30 minutes before serving. Cover and keep cool.
Freezing: freeze the waffles up to 2 weeks before. Refresh and cool as above.

Salmon caviar blinis

If you want to scale these tiny blinis up in size to serve as a first course, then this recipe will make four. I sometimes serve three blinis for each person, separately topped with Chunky Pesto (page 43), Olive & Parsley Salad (page 42) and this salmon caviar topping. MAKES 14-16

for the blinis
4oz/110g boiling potato, quartered
1 egg, separated
1 tblsp double cream [heavy cream]
1 heaped tblsp self-raising flour
  [self-rising flour]
Grated nutmeg
Salt & freshly ground black pepper
Vegetable oil, for greasing
for the topping
2 tblsp crème fraîche
2oz/50g salmon caviar
2 tsp diced red onion
1 tsp finely snipped chives

Cook the quartered potato in a pan of salted water for 15-20 minutes until tender. Drain and purée whilst still hot, using a mouli-legumes, ricer or a sieve.
Mix the potato, egg yolk, cream, flour and seasoning together to make a thick batter. Whisk the egg white until stiff but not dry and fold it into the potato batter.
Grease the frying pan and place it over a moderate heat. Cook teaspoons of the batter for about 1 minute on each side until golden. Lift onto a wire rack to cool.
Spoon the crème fraîche onto the blinis, top with the salmon caviar and sprinkle over the red onion and chives. Serve.

Advance preparation: make the blinis, dice the onion and snip the chives 1 day ahead, cover and chill. Top the blinis up to 2 hours ahead, cover and chill.
Freezing: freeze the blinis 2 weeks before. Refresh at 350°F/180°C/Gas 4 for 2-3 minutes. Cool before serving.

Spicy dahl cakes with avocado relish

These crisp, spicy Indian lentil cakes are topped with a cooling avocado and tomato relish. MAKES 10

for the spicy dahl cakes
4½oz/125g split red lentils
1 hot green chilli, finely chopped
1 small clove garlic, crushed
1½ tsp finely grated ginger
½ tsp asafoetida powder
½ tsp salt
Vegetable oil, for frying
for the avocado relish
1 small plum or salad tomato, peeled,
  seeded & roughly chopped
¼ avocado, roughly chopped
2 spring onions, thinly sliced
2 tsp lemon juice
Salt & freshly ground black pepper

Cover the lentils with cold water and leave to soak for 8 hours.
Drain the lentils and blend them in a food processor with the chilli, garlic, ginger, asafoetida and salt, for about 1 minute, to make a rough, thick paste.
Divide the lentil mixture into 10, flatten and shape into cakes. Fry the cakes in batches in hot oil over a moderate heat for 3-4 minutes on each side, until crisp and golden. Drain and cool on paper towels.
Mix the chopped tomato with the avocado, spring onions and lemon juice, adding salt and pepper to taste.
Spoon the relish on top of the dahl cakes and serve.

Advance preparation: make the dahl cakes up to 12 hours before and store in an airtight container. Make the relish and top the dahl cakes 1 hour before, cover.
Freezing: freeze the dahl cakes 2 weeks ahead. Refresh at 350°F/180°C/Gas 4 for 2-3 minutes. Cool.

Corn fritters with grilled corn & red pepper relish

Corn fritters are very easy to make. The smoky flavour is achieved by searing the corn on a cast-iron grill-pan. I find the relish very handy and also use it in a Thanksgiving sandwich (page 68). MAKES 15

for the corn fritters
1½ ears sweetcorn
3½oz/90g self-raising flour [⅔ cup
  self-rising flour]
1 egg, lightly beaten
4 tblsp milk
1 tsp olive oil
2 tblsp chopped coriander [cilantro]
1 tsp finely diced hot red chilli
3-4 tblsp vegetable oil, for frying
for the grilled corn & red pepper relish
½ ear sweetcorn
½ small red onion, finely diced
½ small red sweet pepper, finely diced
2 tsp chopped sage
1 tblsp lime juice
1 tblsp olive oil
Salt & freshly ground black pepper

Grill the corn, for both the fritters and the relish, on a very hot ridged cast-iron grill-pan, for about 10 minutes, turning it often, until nicely charred. Leave to cool.
Slice the corn kernels off the cobs. Put two-thirds of the kernels into a bowl and the rest into another.
Stir the ingredients for the relish into the smaller amount of corn and season.
Sift the flour for the fritters into a bowl. Make a well in the centre, stir in the egg, milk and olive oil to make a thick batter. Add the remaining corn, coriander, chilli and seasoning and mix well.
Fry small spoonfuls of the batter in a pan of hot oil over a moderate heat for 3-4 minutes on either side, until golden. Drain and cool on paper towels.
Top the fritters with the relish and serve.

Advance preparation: make the corn relish and the corn fritters up to 1 day ahead, cover and chill. Top the fritters with the relish up to 2 hours before, cover and keep cool.
Freezing: not suitable.

Herbed brioche sandwiches

This pretty sandwich is perfect for weddings, christenings and dainty afternoon teas. You can squeeze a little lemon juice into bought mayonnaise to boost its flavour. MAKES 12

4 x ¼in/1cm thick slices brioche
1 rounded tblsp lemon mayonnaise
1 tblsp finely snipped chives
1 tblsp finely chopped dill
1 tsp chive flowers, or similar
You will also need a 2in/5cm plain cutter

Stamp out 10 circles from the brioche but do not include the crust.
Spread a thin coat of mayonnaise on the edge of each circle of brioche, taking care not to get mayonnaise on the top surface.
Mix the herbs together and roll the coated edges of the brioche in this mixture.
Shake gently to remove any excess herbs, arrange on a plate and serve.

Advance preparation: make 2 hours before, cover well with a clean, damp cloth and plastic wrap and chill.
Freezing: not suitable.

Curried lobster sandwich

I know that an open lobster sandwich is not everyone's idea of fast food, but if you have bought the lobster and the mayonnaise, this is a 10 minute recipe. MAKES 10

5 thick slices sourdough or rye bread
5 rounded tblsp mayonnaise
2½ tsp mild curry paste
15oz/425g cooked lobster meat, cubed
1½oz/40g mixed salad leaves, such as
  mizuna, mustard greens or red chard
Salt & freshly ground black pepper
You will also need a 3in/7.5cm round cutter

Stamp out 10 circles from the bread but do not include the crust.
Stir the mayonnaise, curry paste and seasoning together and toss in the lobster. Mix well but carefully.
Divide the salad leaves between the bread and top with the lobster. Serve.

Advance preparation: make the curry mayonnaise 2 days before, cover and chill. Assemble the sandwich 30 minutes before serving, cover and chill.
Freezing: not suitable.

Parmesan, rocket & salsa verde sandwiches

I thought that since the ubiquitous parmesan cheese and rocket salad is such a marvellous combination, I would make a sandwich from them, adding a generous dollop of bright green, peppery salsa verde. The sauce is also wonderful stirred into hot pasta or served as an accompaniment to ham. MAKES 10

1½oz/40g [3 tblsp] unsalted butter,
  softened
6 thin slices white country bread, such as
  pugliese or sourdough, crust removed
3oz/75g parmesan, shaved
1oz/25g rocket [arugula] leaves
for the salsa verde
1½oz/40g rocket [arugula] leaves
½oz/15g [⅓ cup] basil leaves
½oz/15g [⅓ cup] flat-leaf parsley
1 tsp Dijon mustard
1 tsp capers
1½ tblsp olive oil
Salt & freshly ground black pepper

Make the salsa verde by pulsing the rocket, basil and parsley leaves together in a food processor 6-7 times until roughly chopped. Add the rest of the sauce ingredients and blend for 30 seconds to make a rough paste.
Butter the bread on one side only. Divide the salsa verde between 3 slices and spread it to the edges.
Layer the parmesan and rocket leaves on top and cover with the remaining bread.
Press down lightly, cut each sandwich into 4 squares and serve.

Advance preparation: make the salsa verde up to 4 days ahead, cover with a film of olive oil and chill. Pour off the oil before using. Make the sandwiches 2 hours before, cover with a clean, damp cloth and plastic wrap and chill.
Freezing: not suitable.

Toasted brioche with crème fraîche & caviar

Not strictly a sandwich, more an assembly of ingredients, this indulgent recipe is for those times when you are feeling particularly generous towards your friends. Simply lay out the ingredients and let everyone make their own. MAKES 10

5floz/150ml crème fraîche
1 tblsp finely snipped chives
4oz/110g Sevruga caviar
10 x ½in/1cm slices brioche

Mix the crème fraîche and chives together and place in a serving bowl. Spoon the caviar carefully into another bowl.
Cut the brioche into 2in/5cm squares. Place them on a baking tray and lightly toast under the grill [broiler] for about 30 seconds on either side.
Arrange the warm brioche in stacks on a plate and serve with the chive-flavoured crème fraîche and the caviar.

Advance preparation: toast the brioche up to 30 minutes before, leave on the baking tray, cool and cover. Warm briefly under a grill [broiler] before serving.
Freezing: not suitable.

Garlic prawn baguettes

Hot crusty bread filled with garlicky prawns: no one can resist them. Serve a bottle of Tabasco alongside for those who like prawns with piquancy. MAKES 10

10 mini baguettes
1 x Garlic Butter Recipe (page 39)
1½ tblsp lemon juice
1lb10oz/740g cooked shelled prawns
  or shrimps
1 bottle Tabasco sauce

Cut a thin slice from the top of the baguettes and discard. Remove most of the crumb from inside.
Warm the garlic butter with the lemon juice and stir in the prawns or shrimps.
Heat the oven to 350°F/180°C/Gas 4. Divide the garlicky prawns between the baguettes, place on a baking tray and

bake for 10-15 minutes until piping hot. Serve with a bottle of Tabasco sauce for guests to add to the baguettes as desired.

Advance preparation: fill the baguettes 2 hours before, cover and chill. Heat as above.
Freezing: freeze the garlic butter 4 weeks before.

Italian BLT focaccia

This Italian BLT with hot pancetta is a twist on the classic BLT sandwich. MAKES 10

10 yellow or red tomatoes, halved lengthways
7floz/210ml olive oil
A large pinch of sugar
20 slices pancetta, or thinly cut bacon
10 x 4in/10cm squares herbed focaccia, split
1lb2oz/500g [2 cups] ricotta cheese
1½oz/40g [1 cup] purple or green basil leaves
Salt & freshly ground black pepper

Heat the oven to 190°C/375°F/Gas 5. Put the tomatoes skin-side down in a roasting pan, drizzle with 4 tblsp of the olive oil and sprinkle with the sugar plus some salt and pepper.
Roast the tomatoes for 30 minutes or until soft and slightly charred. Remove from the pan whilst warm, lift onto paper towels and leave to cool.
Dry-fry the pancetta for 2-3 minutes or until very crisp. Drain and cool on paper towels.
Drizzle the cut surfaces of the focaccia with the remaining olive oil. Cover with the pancetta.
Spread on the ricotta, add the tomatoes, then the basil. Put the lids on and serve.

Advance preparation: roast, cool and chill the tomatoes up to 2 days before. Fry the pancetta 1 day before, cover and chill. Make the sandwiches 2 hours ahead, cover and chill.
Freezing: the pancetta can be cooked and frozen up to 4 weeks ahead. Crisp up in a preheated oven at 375°F/190°C/Gas 5 for 3-4 minutes. Cool before serving.

left Italian BLT focaccia

Bagels with red pepper & olive relish

Bagels with red pepper & olive relish

Bagels with smoked salmon and cream cheese are a winner, but they are also good spread with mascarpone and this relish. MAKES 10

3 red sweet peppers
5 bagels, split
5oz/150g [1 cup] pitted black olives, roughly chopped
2½oz/60g capers in balsamic vinegar
5 tblsp roughly chopped flat-leaf parsley
2 tblsp olive oil
9floz/250ml [1 cup] mascarpone
Salt & freshly ground black pepper

Grill [broil] the peppers until the skins are blackened. Place in a bowl, cover with plastic wrap and stand for 10 minutes.
Peel and seed the peppers, set the flesh aside to cool, then chop it roughly.
Toast both sides of the bagels lightly and leave to cool.

Mix the chopped peppers with the olives, capers, parsley and olive oil, then season.
Spread the mascarpone on the cut side of the bagels, spoon on the red pepper and olive relish and serve.

Advance preparation: make the relish 3 days ahead without the parsley; cover and chill. Top the bagels 1 hour before.
Freezing: not suitable.

Soft-shell crab sandwich & courgette fries

Crabs and shoestring fries crammed between slices of black rye bread are sheer bliss! The fries and crab can be served individually but you will need lots of napkins. MAKES 10

4½oz/125g water biscuits or plain crackers
20 slices black rye bread
Vegetable oil, for frying
Salt & freshly ground black pepper

for the tartare sauce
5 rounded tblsp mayonnaise
2 rounded tblsp roughly chopped pickled dill cucumbers or gherkins
1 rounded tblsp roughly chopped parsley
1 small red onion, finely chopped
1 rounded tblsp finely snipped chives
2 rounded tsp capers
for the courgette fries
1lb/450g courgettes [zucchini]
3 tblsp plain flour [all-purpose flour]
for the soft-shell crabs
3 tblsp plain flour [all-purpose flour]
10 x 4oz/110g soft-shell crabs
2 medium eggs, lightly beaten
A few drops of Tabasco sauce

Mix all the ingredients together for the tartare sauce and season.
Pulse the crackers in a food processor 7-8 times to make rough crumbs.
Spread the tartare sauce over 10 slices of the rye bread.
Cut the courgettes into ⅛in/3mm thick sticks, ideally using a mandoline. Toss them in flour with lots of seasoning.
Season the flour for the crabs and then toss them in this mixture to coat well.
Mix the eggs and Tabasco together, dip the crabs in to coat and then roll them in the cracker crumbs.
Heat a large pan of oil for deep-frying to 300°F/150°C and heat the oven to 350°F/180°C/Gas 4. Deep-fry the crab in batches in the hot oil for 3 minutes until crisp and golden brown. Drain on paper towels and keep warm in the oven.
Deep-fry the courgettes in batches in the oil for 1 minute or until crisp and golden, stirring constantly. Drain them on paper towels and sprinkle with salt. Keep warm.
Put a soft-shell crab on top of each piece of sauced bread, add the courgette fries and top with the remaining slices of bread. Serve immediately.

Advance preparation: make the tartare sauce and the biscuit crumbs up to 2 days before. Cover and chill the sauce and store the crumbs in an airtight container. Cut the fries up to 4 hours ahead, cover and chill. Fry to order.
Freezing: not suitable.

Muffuletta

Muffuletta is native to New Orleans. It is a macho, chunky sandwich, great for picnics, or for when you know that your guests will have demanding and hearty appetites. You can also fill individual rolls, such as ciabatta, with these layers of salami, cheese and olive salad. SERVES 10

11oz/315g [2 cups] pitted black olives, roughly chopped
2 large roasted red sweet peppers (see left), peeled, seeded & roughly chopped or 10oz/275g [1½ cups] drained canned red pimientos, rinsed & roughly chopped
1 large clove garlic, crushed
5floz/150ml olive oil
1 tblsp lemon juice
2 x 14oz/400g rustic round loaves bread, flavoured with olives, tomato or cheese
5oz/150g salami, sliced
2oz/50g curly endive
12oz/350g taleggio or mozzarella, sliced
5oz/150g mortadella, sliced
2oz/50g rocket [arugula] leaves
Freshly ground black pepper

Combine the olives, peppers, garlic, olive oil, lemon juice and black pepper.

Cut the breads across the middle and remove the crumb from both the top and bottom halves. (Reserve and freeze the crumb for another recipe.)

Divide half the olive mixture between the bottom of each loaf and, in the following order, arrange the salami, curly endive, taleggio or mozzarella, the rest of the olive mixture, mortadella and rocket, in layers inside them.

Replace the bread lids, cover with plastic wrap and chill for at least 1 hour before serving. Divide each of the muffuletta into 5 wedges and serve.

Advance preparation: make the olive mixture 3 days ahead but do not add the lemon juice until assembling; cover and chill. Fill the bread up to 6 hours before, cover and chill.
Freezing: not suitable.

right Soft-shell crab sandwich & courgette fries

Thanksgiving roll with sweet potato fries

Thanksgiving usually means roast turkey, sweet potatoes, cornbread stuffing and cranberry sauce. Here I am celebrating Thanksgiving, not traditionally, but instead served in a roll. There is turkey and grilled corn relish inside and some chunky sweet potato fries served as a side order. I have never been a fan of cranberry sauce, but if it is an essential part of Thanksgiving for you, go ahead and add some. MAKES 10

2lb/900g roasted turkey, sliced
10 soft brown rolls, halved
5 rounded tblsp mayonnaise
A few leaves of curly endive
1 x Grilled Corn and Red Pepper Relish Recipe (page 63)
3 rounded tblsp cranberry sauce (optional)
for the sweet potato fries
2½lb/1.15kg sweet potatoes, unpeeled & cut into chunky fries
Vegetable oil, for deep-frying
Salt

Heat the oven to 375°F/190°C/Gas 5. Spread the turkey slices out on an oven-proof dish and warm them in the oven for 12-15 minutes or until piping hot.

Wash and dry the sweet potatoes very well. Heat the oil in a deep-fat fryer to 300°F/150°C. Fry the sweet potatoes in batches for 4 minutes until cooked. Drain on paper towels and then fry again for a further minute, again in batches, until crisp and golden. Drain on paper towels and lightly salt. Keep warm.

Thanksgiving roll with sweet potato fries

Spread the rolls with mayonnaise, divide the endive between them, put the turkey on top and finish with some relish or cranberry sauce. Replace the tops of the rolls and serve them with the hot fries.

Advance preparation: make the corn relish up to 1 day before, cover and chill. Cut the fries up to 2 hours before and fry them up to 1 hour ahead for 4 minutes. Drain. Refry for 1 minute to order. *Freezing: not suitable.*

Sloppy Joe pitta breads

Here the American favourite, Sloppy Joes, are given a Tex-Mex feel. Typically served in toasted burger buns, I have swapped them for pitta breads as the pockets make natural containers for the spicy beef. You will have to fill the Sloppy Joes to order, otherwise the bread gets too soft, then wrap them in a napkin or some waxed paper, as they make a real mess and will spill all over the place. They are great filling party food but not dainty eating! MAKES 10

10 x 4in/10cm pitta breads
for the beef mixture
1 medium onion, chopped
1½ tblsp jalapeño chilli, unseeded, finely chopped
1 large clove garlic, crushed
4 tblsp vegetable oil
1½lb/700g minced [ground] beef
1 tblsp ground cumin
14oz/400g canned chopped tomatoes
5floz/150ml tomato ketchup
Salt & freshly ground black pepper
for the topping
2 x Avocado Relish Recipe (page 63)
1 hot red chilli, finely diced
5floz/150ml sour cream

Sauté the onion, chilli and garlic together in oil in a large frying pan over a medium heat for about 7-8 minutes or until soft and translucent.

Add the beef and cook over a high heat for 4-5 minutes, stirring all the time, until lightly browned. Drain off and discard all the fat. Add the cumin and seasoning and cook for 1 minute.

Reduce the heat to medium and add the canned tomatoes and ketchup. Season and cook for 20-30 minutes until the mixture is thick but still sloppy.

Add the diced chilli to the avocado relish. Cut the tops off the pitta breads.

Spoon the beef mixture into the pitta breads, top with a dollop of sour cream and the avocado relish. Wrap in a napkin and serve immediately.

Advance preparation: make the beef mixture 2 days before, cool, cover and chill. Reheat in a pan for 15-20 minutes until piping hot. Make the avocado relish up to 1 hour before and cover.
Freezing: the beef mixture can be frozen up to 4 weeks ahead. Reheat as above.

Right: *give those old-fashioned food favourites a twist – these lip-smacking, spicy wedges are made from potatoes and served with a tamarind-flavoured ketchup for dipping.* **Below:** *when there is no room in the fridge, keep beers and other bottled drinks cold by piling them in buckets filled with ice. Your local wine merchant is the best source of bulk ice – they usually rent glasses for parties too.*

Left: *garlic bread is perennially popular. Here it is piled high with juicy warm prawns or shrimp for a hearty hand-held snack.* **Right:** *it is not necessary to continually walk round the party offering finger items to guests. Spread platters of food out on a simply decorated table that you have moved to one side of the room and let guests serve themselves. Make sure there is plenty of space around the table.*

housewarming

Above: *elegance is not always desired, especially at informal events, so for a housewarming make some finger food that is hot and hearty. Pile beef chilli into pitta bread pockets, then top with sour cream, garnish with avocado relish and wrap in a colourful napkin for a snack that really soaks up the beer.*

Left: *a new take on crudités. Crisp vegetables and shellfish are matched with a creamy bean dip.*

Left: *the clever party host will make use of good things from favourite takeaways and food stores. Here, bottled chutneys and pickles are served with poppadoms from an Indian restaurant.* Above: *muffuletta, a loaf of bread filled with Italian deli items, is easy to make, filling and tasty.* Right: *chicken wings are easy to nibble on held with the fingers. Give them a spicy treatment with red curry paste.*

Seeded potato croquettes with balsamic dip

These crisp cylinders of seeded potato can be cooked before the party and reheated in the oven to avoid last-minute frying. MAKES 10

9oz/250g boiling potatoes, quartered
2oz/50g [½ cup] parmesan, grated
3 spring onions [scallions], thinly sliced
1 egg, lightly beaten
1oz/25g [3 tblsp] toasted sesame seeds
1oz/25g [3 tblsp] toasted pumpkin seeds
1oz/25g [3 tblsp] toasted sunflower seeds
Vegetable oil, for frying
4 tblsp balsamic vinegar
Salt & freshly ground black pepper

Cook the potatoes in a pan of salted water for 15-20 minutes until tender. Drain and purée whilst still hot, using a mouli-legumes, ricer or sieve (a food processor will make the potato gluey).
Stir in the parmesan, spring onions and seasoning and shape into 10 croquettes.
Mix all the seeds together on a plate. Dip the croquettes in the beaten egg and then roll them in the seeds to coat.
Heat a pan of oil for deep-frying to 350°F/180°C. Deep-fry the croquettes in batches for 1½ minutes until golden. Drain on paper towels. Serve immediately with a bowl of balsamic vinegar to dip.

Advance preparation: make the potato and cheese mixture 2 days before, cover and chill. Fry the croquettes 4 hours before, cover and chill. Reheat in the oven at 350°F/180°C/Gas 4 for 7-8 minutes.
Freezing: not suitable.

Deep-fried sage leaves with anchovies

These salty anchovy-filled sage leaves also make an excellent crispy garnish for fish dishes, particularly risottos. MAKES 20

10 anchovy fillets, split lengthways
40 large sage leaves
2 medium eggs, lightly beaten
2oz/50g plain flour [⅓ cup all-purpose flour]
Salt & freshly ground black pepper

Sandwich a halved anchovy fillet between 2 sage leaves, keeping the smooth side of the leaves outermost. Repeat until all the leaves are used up.
Dip the stuffed sage leaves into the egg and then into seasoned flour.
Heat the oil to 425°F/220°C and deep-fry for 1 minute until crisp and golden. Drain on paper towels and serve immediately.

Advance preparation: prepare the stuffed sage leaves to the stage of frying 1 hour before and cover. Fry to order.
Freezing: not suitable.

Vermicelli prawns on Chinese seaweed

These fat prawns, covered with vermicelli and deep-fried, have the appearance of spiky hedgehogs. Serve on crispy Chinese seaweed, with some chopsticks to gather up the elusive strands. The 'seaweed', beloved of every Chinese restaurant, is not seaweed at all, but finely shredded bok choy or spring greens, deep-fried and tossed in a mixture of sugar and salt. MAKES 10

Vegetable oil, for deep frying
Chinese plum sauce, to serve
for the seaweed
12oz/350g bok choy, spring greens, collards or spinach
½ tsp sugar
½ tsp salt
for the vermicelli prawns
10 large raw tiger prawns, peeled
2 tsp cornflour [cornstarch]
1 small egg, beaten
3 tblsp vermicelli, broken into small pieces
Salt & freshly ground black pepper

Heat the oven to 325°F/170°C/Gas 3. Trim and discard the stalk from the greens. Roll 2 or 3 of the leaves together and shred them finely with a sharp knife. Repeat with the remaining leaves.
Separate the strips and spread them out on baking trays. Place in the oven for about 10 minutes to dry out slightly. Meanwhile, heat a large pan of oil for deep-frying to 350°F/180°C.

Cool the shredded greens, then deep-fry in batches for about 30 seconds or until crisp. Do not overcook them or they will taste bitter. Drain on paper towels.
Add the sugar and salt to the greens and toss well. Return the greens to the oven to keep warm.
Toss the prawns in seasoned cornflour, then in the egg and finally in vermicelli.
Deep-fry in batches for 2 minutes at 350°F/180°C or until the vermicelli has puffed up and the prawns are cooked.
Drain on paper towels and serve on the seaweed with a bowl of plum sauce to dip.

Advance preparation: fry the seaweed up to 8 hours before and store in an airtight container. Warm in a preheated oven at 325°F/170°C/Gas 3 for 5 minutes until hot. Fry the prawns to order.
Freezing: not suitable.

Fish & chips

Miniature portions of fish and chips, served in newspaper cones lined with greaseproof paper, are one of our most regularly requested canapés. Offer vinegar separately, but make sure that the vinegar is malt – wine vinegar is just a bit too smart. MAKES 10

8oz/225g potatoes, cut into thin chips, or frozen French fries
7oz/200g haddock or cod fillet, cut into 10
3oz/75g squid, cut into rings (optional)
4oz/110g whitebait
3 tblsp plain flour [all-purpose flour]
Vegetable oil, for frying
Malt vinegar, to serve
Salt & freshly ground black pepper
for the batter
2oz/50g plain flour [⅓ cup all-purpose flour], sifted
2 tsp olive oil
3½floz/100ml water
1 egg white
You will also need 10 cones of paper lined with greaseproof or waxed paper

Make the batter by making a well in the flour and gradually whisking in the oil and water to give a thick mixture. Season with salt, cover and let it rest for 1 hour.

Rinse the chips in cold water and dry thoroughly on paper towels.

Whisk the egg white until stiff but not dry and then fold it into the batter.

Heat a large pan of vegetable oil for deep-frying to 350°F/180°C and set the oven to 350°F/180°C/Gas 4.

Dip the haddock or cod into the batter and deep-fry for about 4 minutes until crisp and golden. Drain on paper towels then keep warm in the hot oven.

Toss the squid and whitebait in seasoned flour and fry in the hot oil for 1-2 minutes until golden. Drain on paper towels and keep warm in the oven.

Fry the chips for 3-4 minutes. Drain on paper towels and then fry them again for a further minute until crisp and golden. Drain on paper towels.

Toss all the fish and chips together and season with salt. Pile into the newspaper cones and serve immediately with vinegar.

Advance preparation: cut the chips, leave them in cold water and cover, up to 4 hours before. Make the batter, without adding the egg white, up to 4 hours ahead and cover. Fry everything to order.
Freezing: not suitable

Fish & chips

Prawns & sugar cane skewers

Now, I know that most people do not have easy access to fresh sugar cane but some enlightened supermarkets stock it, as do West Indian and Asian food markets. Seek it out if you can, as it does impart a lovely flavour to this prawn mixture. It is also nice to chew on. Otherwise, just mould the mixture onto sticks of lemongrass or bamboo skewers instead. MAKES 10

2ft/60cm length fresh sugar cane
Vegetable oil, for deep-frying
Sweet chilli sauce, to serve
for the prawn mixture
6oz/175g raw prawns or shrimps
4oz/110g water chestnuts
1 small clove garlic, crushed
2 tsp finely grated ginger
1 tsp finely chopped lemongrass
½ medium egg white
1 tblsp plain flour [all-purpose flour]
   + extra for moulding
Salt & freshly ground black pepper

Use a cleaver to chop the sugar cane into 6in/15cm lengths, then carefully chop away and discard all the hard outer bark to reveal the moist sugar cane inside. Cut each piece into 5 sticks measuring ¼in/5mm x 6in/15cm.

Put all the ingredients for the prawn mixture in a food processor and pulse 5-6 times until chopped and combined.

Divide the prawn mixture into 10 and, using floured hands, mould around the sugar cane, or on the alternative skewers.

Heat a large pan of oil for deep-frying to 300°F/150°C. Deep-fry the skewers in batches for 4 minutes or until cooked and golden. Drain on paper towels. Serve hot with a bowl of chilli sauce to dip.

Advance preparation: mould the prawn mixture on the sugar cane up to 4 hours ahead, cover and chill. Fry to order.
Freezing: not suitable.

Bay scallops with Thai dipping sauce

I love this simple fishy canapé with its pert flavours of coriander and pickled ginger. The dipping sauce is also excellent as a dressing for chicken or fish salads. MAKES 20

for the Thai dipping sauce
2 tblsp Thai fish sauce
1 tblsp lime juice
2 tblsp palm sugar, or dark brown sugar
1 red bird's-eye chilli, finely sliced
1 spring onion [scallion], finely sliced
2 tsp finely sliced red onion
2 tsp finely chopped cucumber
2 tsp finely chopped carrot
2 tsp chopped peanuts
for the scallops
20 bay scallops
20 coriander [cilantro] leaves
20 pieces pickled ginger
Sesame oil, for greasing
You will also need 20 toothpicks

Make the dipping sauce by combining all the ingredients and stirring until the sugar has dissolved. Pour into a small bowl.
Heat a ridged cast-iron grill-pan and grease it lightly with the sesame oil. Sear the scallops on both sides, for about 2-3 minutes in total. Remove to some paper towels to cool. Alternatively, light a charcoal fire and cook the scallops on an oiled rack set 4-6in/10-15cm above medium-hot coals for 2-3 minutes on each side, then cool on paper towels.
Skewer the scallops on the toothpicks with the coriander leaves and pickled ginger and serve with the dipping sauce.

Advance preparation: make the dipping sauce up to 2 days ahead, cover and chill. Cook the scallops up to 4 hours before, cover and chill. Assemble 1 hour before serving, cover and chill.
Freezing: not suitable.

Italian vegetable skewers

Mix and match the vegetables on these skewers – they do not have to be identical. If you like, offer them with a pesto dip, or brush with pesto before serving. MAKES 10

6 bocconcini (tiny mozzarella)
6 sun-dried tomato halves in oil
6 yellow or red plum cherry tomatoes

3 yellow or green pattypan squash, halved
½ small red or yellow sweet pepper, cut into 8
3 baby courgettes [zucchini], cut into 2in/5cm pieces
3 spring onions [scallions], cut into 2in/5cm pieces
1 small red onion, cut into 6 wedges through the root

Italian vegetable skewers

4 tblsp olive oil + extra for greasing
2 cloves garlic, crushed
Salt & freshly ground black pepper
You will also need 10 bamboo skewers

Soak the skewers in a bowl of water for
2 hours. This will stop them burning.
Marinate all the ingredients in the oil,
garlic and seasoning for 30 minutes.

Thread a mixture of the bocconcini and
5 different vegetables onto each skewer.
Cook on a hot ridged cast-iron grill-pan
or under the grill [broiler] for 5-7 minutes,
turning once or twice, until the vegetables
are tender but still have some bite.
Alternatively, place the skewers on an
oiled rack set 4in/10cm above medium-
hot charcoal. Turn them after 5 minutes

or so and cook for a further 5 minutes,
until done. Serve the skewers hot or cold.

Advance preparation: marinate the
cheese and vegetables up to 12 hours
before, cover and chill. If serving the
skewers cold, cook them up to 6 hours
in advance, cover and chill.
Freezing: not suitable.

Sticky red curry chicken wings

*Sticky and shiny fire-engine red, these
Thai-flavoured chicken wings can be
barbecued or roasted.* MAKES 10

4oz/110g [½ cup] palm sugar, or dark
  brown sugar
4oz/110g [½ cup] tomato paste
2oz/50g [¼ cup] Thai red curry paste
2 tsp salt
10 chicken wings
Vegetable oil, for greasing

Heat the palm sugar and tomato paste in
a pan over a low heat for 4-5 minutes or
until the sugar has dissolved.
Remove from the heat, stir in the curry
paste and salt and leave to cool.
Pour the cooled mixture over the chicken
wings and toss well to coat. Cover and
marinate in the fridge for at least 4 hours.
Heat the oven to 375°F/190°C/Gas 5.
Transfer the chicken wings to a lightly
oiled roasting pan and spread them out.
Roast the wings for 35-40 minutes until
cooked and slightly charred. Alternatively,
place them wings on an oiled rack
4-6in/10-15cm above medium-hot
charcoal and cook for 12-15 minutes,
turning once. Serve hot or cold.

Advance preparation: cook, cover and
chill up to 1 day before. If serving the
wings hot, reheat at 375°F/190°C/Gas 5
for 20 minutes until piping hot.
*Freezing: freeze the cooked chicken
wings up to 4 weeks before. Reheat as
above, or defrost and serve cold.*

Passionfruit & papaya won-tons

Won-ton wrappers need not be restricted to savoury foods; they are just as good with sweet toppings like tropical fruits. Dusted with icing sugar and cinnamon, they are also an easy accompaniment for desserts such as Kissel (page 132), or granita. MAKES 10

Vegetable oil, for deep-frying
10 won-ton wrappers
1 rounded tblsp fromage frais or blanc
¼ small papaya, thinly sliced
2 passionfruit, seeds & juice removed
Icing sugar [confectioners' sugar],
  for dusting

Heat the oil in a pan to 350°F/180°C and fry the won-ton wrappers for about 30 seconds until golden brown. Drain well on kitchen paper and cool.
Top each fried won-ton wrapper with a little of the fromage frais, a few slices of papaya and some passionfruit seeds.
Dust the won-tons with icing sugar and serve immediately.

Advance preparation: fry the wrappers up to 12 hours in advance and store in an airtight container. Prepare the fruits 3-4 hours before serving, cover and chill. *Freezing: not suitable.*

Elderflower jellies

Bottled elderflower cordial makes beautifully scented, pop-in-the-mouth jellies that I have studded with fresh berries. MAKES 20

6 leaves gelatine
7 tblsp boiling water
5½floz/165ml elderflower cordial
10 raspberries
20 blueberries
You will also need 2 trays of 10 ice-cubes

Soak the gelatine in some cold water for 10 minutes, then squeeze it to remove the excess water.
Put the measured boiling water into a jug, add the gelatine and stir until dissolved. Pour in the elderflower cordial, stir and leave to cool for 10 minutes.

Divide the raspberries between one of the ice-cube trays and the blueberries between the other. Pour the elderflower mixture over these fruits and then chill for 5 hours or until set.
Dip the ice-cube trays in very hot water, just up to the level of the jelly, count to 5 and remove from the water.
Use a small sharp knife to loosen the edges of the jellies and turn out onto a plate lined with plastic wrap. Transfer the jellies to a serving dish using a palette knife [metal spatula].

Fruited bruschetta

Advance preparation: make the jellies up to 2 days ahead, cover and chill. *Freezing: not suitable.*

Fruited bruschetta

You can use all different types of breads and toppings for sweet bruschetta. Try chocolate bread with coffee ice-cream drizzled with chocolate sauce or maple syrup. A spoonful of Red Berry Kissel (page 132) with a dollop of Lemon Syllabub (page 81) is also a glorious combination. MAKES 20

for the strawberry, raspberry & peach bruschetta

10 slices brioche, cut from individual brioche

4oz/110g [½ cup] clotted cream or mascarpone

1 peach, thinly sliced

10 strawberries, thinly sliced

3oz/75g [¾ cup] raspberries

for the mango & passionfruit bruschetta

10 slices fruit bread

5floz/150ml double cream [heavy cream], lightly whipped

3 passionfruit, seeds & juice removed

1 small mango, thinly sliced

A small piece of fresh coconut, unskinned

Toast the slices of brioche and fruited bread lightly on either side under a preheated grill [broiler] or on a ridged cast-iron grill-pan. Leave to cool.

Spoon the clotted cream or mascarpone onto the brioche and arrange the peaches, strawberries and raspberries on top.

Mix the whipped cream with the seeds and juice of one passionfruit and spoon it onto the fruit bread. Top the cream with the mango and the seeds and juice of the remaining passionfruit.

Make fine shavings of coconut using a vegetable peeler and arrange them on top of the fruit before serving.

Advance preparation: toast the breads and keep covered, add the passionfruit to the cream, slice the peaches and strawberries and chill 1-2 hours ahead. Top the bruschetta 30 minutes before. *Freezing: not suitable.*

Summer berry tartlets

Strained Greek yogurt or mascarpone topped with tropical fruit makes a good alternative to the clotted cream and red berries in these tartlets. The fail-safe pastry recipe given here can be used for a number of sweet dishes. It is not worth making smaller amounts of the dough, so divide it into batches and freeze for use as required. This recipe will yield 2lb/900g of sweet pastry which in turn will make: 120 x 1½in/4cm mini tartlets; 20 x 4in/10cm shallow tarts; or 3 x 10in/25.5cm large shallow tarts. To make savoury pastry, simply omit the sugar. MAKES 12

for the sweet shortcrust pastry (makes 2lb/900g)
1lb/450g plain flour [3 cups all-purpose flour], sifted + extra for dusting

5oz/150g icing sugar [1¼ cups confectioners' sugar], sifted
A pinch of salt
8oz/225g [1 cup] unsalted butter, diced
1 egg, beaten
1 tblsp cold water
for the filling
3½floz/100ml [½ cup] clotted cream
8oz/225g selection of berries, such as blackberries, halved strawberries, raspberries, and red or blackcurrants
A few sprigs of mint, to decorate, if using strawberries
Icing sugar [confectioners' sugar], for dusting
You will also need a set of 12 tartlet tins 1½in/4cm in diameter and a 2in/5cm round cutter

French apple tartlets

Put the flour, icing sugar, salt and butter together in a food processor and pulse 7-8 times until the mixture resembles fine breadcrumbs. Turn into a bowl, add the egg and water and mix with a palette knife [metal spatula].

Knead well to make a firm dough. Wrap 4oz/110g [about ⅛] of the pastry in plastic wrap and chill for 30 minutes before using; freeze the remainder in batches for use in other recipes.

Roll the chilled pastry out thinly on a lightly floured surface and use the cutter to stamp out 12 circles. Carefully line the tartlet tins, pressing the pastry down into the bottom and up the sides of the tins. Trim away any excess, lightly prick the bases with a fork and chill for 30 minutes.

Heat the oven to 375°F/190°C/Gas 5 and bake the tartlets for 10 minutes until golden. Cool for 10 minutes before removing from the tins to a plate.

Fill the tartlet cases with the clotted cream, divide the fruits amongst them, decorating any strawberries with mint leaves, and lightly dust with icing sugar.

Advance preparation: make the pastry 2 days before, cover with plastic wrap and chill. Allow to soften for 20 minutes before using. Bake the tartlet cases 1 day before and store in an airtight container. Fill 45 minutes before serving.
Freezing: freeze the pastry in batches 4 weeks ahead. The baked tartlet cases can be frozen 3 weeks ahead and crisped up in an oven at 350°F/180°C/Gas 4 for 2-3 minutes. Cool before assembling.

French apple tartlets

These are miniature versions of the classic French apple tart. MAKES 12

⅛ (4oz/110g) x Sweet Shortcrust Pastry Recipe (left)
Flour, for dusting
2 small dessert apples, peeled & cored
1 tblsp icing sugar [confectioners' sugar]
You will also need 12 square tartlet tins or a set of 12 round tartlet tins 1½in/4cm in diameter and a 2in/5cm square or round cutter

Roll the pastry out thinly on a lightly floured surface, stamp out 12 squares or circles and use them to line the tartlet tins. Trim away any excess, prick the bases with a fork and chill for 30 minutes.
Heat the oven to 375°F/190°C/Gas 5. Cut the apples into 6 wedges then cut 72 very thin slices from the apples and roughly chop the rest.
Fill the tartlets with the chopped apple and arrange the slices on top. Place on a baking tray and bake for 15 minutes, until the fruit is cooked and the pastry golden.
Dust the top of the tartlets with icing sugar and quickly flash under a hot grill [broiler] to glaze the apple slices.
Cool for 10 minutes, then remove from the tins to a plate. Serve warm or cold.

Advance preparation: 1 day before, line the tartlet tins with pastry, cover and chill. *Freezing: the tartlet cases can be frozen unbaked in their tins for 1 week, then filled and baked straight from the freezer.*

Lemon syllabub puffs

Choux pastry is highly versatile as it can be used for both sweet and savoury foods. As well as this syllabub, clotted cream and red berries, Saffron Cream (page 137), Chunky Pesto (page 43) or lemony crab (page 33) are good fillings to use. MAKES 16

for the choux pastry
3floz/75ml water
1oz/25g [2 tblsp] unsalted butter + extra for greasing
1oz/25g plain flour [3 tblsp all-purpose flour], sifted
A pinch of salt
1 small egg, lightly beaten
for the lemon syllabub
2 tsp lemon juice
2 tsp sherry or brandy
1 tblsp sweet white wine
1 tsp sugar
4½ tblsp double cream [heavy cream]
16 crystallized violets, to decorate
Icing sugar [confectioners' sugar], for dusting
You will also need a piping bag and plain ⅓in/1cm nozzle

Make the choux by gently melting the butter in a saucepan with the water. Then, bring the water to the boil, remove from the heat and tip in the flour and salt.
Return the pan to a low heat and stir the dough vigorously with a wooden spoon for 3-4 minutes until the mixture cleanly leaves the sides of the pan. Cool slightly.
Add the egg to the dough and beat until you have a smooth, glossy mixture.
Heat the oven to 400°F/200°C/Gas 6. Place small spoonfuls of the pastry well apart on a lightly greased baking sheet. Bake for 10-12 minutes until crisp.
Make a small slit in the top of each puff, return to the oven and leave the door ajar for 5 minutes to dry them out.
Cool on a rack and then cut a small wedge from the tops of the puffs.

Lemon syllabub puffs

Mix the lemon juice, sherry and wine together, add the sugar and stir to dissolve. Slowly pour this mixture onto the cream, stirring gently with a small whisk, until it forms soft peaks.
Spoon the syllabub into a piping bag fitted with a nozzle and pipe it into the puffs. Decorate with the violets, lightly dust with icing sugar and serve.

Advance preparation: make the syllabub and puffs 1 day in advance. Cover and chill the syllabub and whisk briefly if it separates. Put the pastries in an airtight box; crisp up for 2-3 minutes at 350°F/180°C/Gas 4 then cool. Fill the puffs up to 1 hour before serving. *Freezing: freeze the baked puffs 3 weeks ahead, crisp up and fill as above.*

Yogurt ices

Desserts do not always have to be grown-up and these frozen yogurt cones are a fun way to end a casual meal. MAKES 20

20 ice-cream cones
for the lemon curd ices
1lb2oz/500g [2 cups] strained plain yogurt
9oz/250g lemon curd, or other fruit curd
2oz/50g candied citrus peel, finely sliced
for the strawberry ices
1lb2oz/500g [2 cups] strained plain yogurt
4oz/110g caster sugar [½ cup granulated sugar]
4oz/110g [⅔ cup] strawberries, hulled & quartered + 10 whole strawberries
You will also need an ice-cream scoop

Whisk the first batch of yogurt and the lemon curd together in a plastic bowl for 2 minutes until light and aerated.
Scrape down the sides of the bowl and freeze for 1 hour. Break up the semi-frozen mixture with a fork, then whisk again for 2 minutes. Scrape down the sides again and freeze for a further hour. Repeat once more, transfer to a lidded container and freeze for at least 4 hours.
Repeat the same procedure for the strawberry ices whisking only the yogurt and sugar together. After the third whisking, add the strawberries, whisk again for 10 seconds, transfer to a lidded container and freeze for at least 4 hours.
Remove the frozen ices from the freezer, allow to soften slightly and make into balls with an ice-cream scoop.
Top 10 of the cones with a scoop of the lemon ice and sprinkle with the citrus peel. Fill the remaining cones with the strawberry ice, then decorate with the strawberries and serve immediately.

Advance preparation: slice the citrus peel up to 1 week ahead and store in an airtight container.
Freezing: make the ices up to 3 weeks ahead and remove from the freezer about 20 minutes before serving.

left Yogurt ices

Ice-cream filled brioche

Chocolate cups with ice-cream

You can buy both the chocolate cases and the ice-creams for an instant, bite-sized indulgence. MAKES 10

7oz/200g [about 1 cup] selection of ice-creams or sorbets, such as chocolate, coffee, orange or vanilla
10 mini chocolate cups
You will also need a melon baller

Make small balls of ice-cream with the melon baller and arrange one in each of the chocolate cups. Serve.

Advance preparation: see below.
Freezing: freeze the filled cups 2 days before in an airtight box. Serve straight from the freezer.

Ice-cream filled brioche

This is another effortless recipe which makes good use of shop-bought items. MAKES 10

10 bite-sized brioche, muffins or cakes
4½oz/125g [heaped ½ cup] ice-cream, such as pistachio or strawberry
Icing sugar [confectioners' sugar], for dusting

Cut the tops off the brioche, hollow them out and then spoon in the ice-cream.
Replace the lids, lightly dust with icing sugar and serve immediately.

Advance preparation: hollow out the brioche 4 hours before and cover.
Freezing: fill 3-4 days in advance and freeze. Let the brioche soften for a few minutes before dusting with icing sugar.

Heart-shaped chocolate cookies

Heart-shaped chocolate cookies

Make these heart-shaped cookies when you are feeling particularly romantic, or to serve at weddings – perhaps giving every guest one as they leave. I find the chocolate cookie dough recipe very useful: this quantity of pastry will also yield approximately 120 x 1¾in/4.5cm mini cookies; 120 x 2in/5cm numerals for decorating birthday cakes or for serving as cookies; or 65 x 2¼in/6.5cm cookies for afternoon tea or to accompany desserts. MAKES 12

for the chocolate cookie dough (makes 1¾lb/800g)
6½oz/185g [13 tblsp] unsalted butter, softened
9½oz/265g caster sugar [1⅓ cups granulated sugar]
1 egg, beaten
7oz/200g plain flour [1⅓ cups all-purpose flour] + extra for rolling
4oz/110g [1¼ cups] unsweetened cocoa powder
A pinch of salt

for the icing
1 egg white, lightly beaten
5oz/150g icing sugar [1¼ cups confectioners' sugar], sifted
You will also need 3 heart-shaped cutters, approximately 4in/10.5cm, 3in/7cm and 2in/5cm wide, a piping bag, an ⅛in/3mm plain nozzle and 12 lengths of 12in/30cm thin ribbon

Beat the butter and caster sugar for the chocolate cookie dough together until light and creamy. Add the egg and beat well for another 1-2 minutes.
Sift in the flour, cocoa and salt and knead to combine. Put the dough into plastic wrap and chill for 1 hour.
Roll the dough out to a thickness of ¼in/5mm on a lightly floured surface. Stamp out 12 hearts using the 4in/10cm cutter and transfer to baking trays.
Use the 3in/7.5cm cutter to stamp out a heart from the centre of each large heart. Transfer these smaller hearts to another baking tray and trim, using the 2in/5cm cutter, so they fit inside the large hearts.
Make a hole large enough to take some thin ribbon in the top of each cookie, using a skewer or a small sharp knife. Chill for 30 minutes.
Heat the oven to 350°F/180°C/Gas 4 and bake the hearts for 8 minutes, until slightly darker in colour. Lift them onto a wire rack to cool.
Beat together the egg white and icing sugar to make the icing. Spoon into a piping bag and decorate the cookies as desired with hearts and lettering.
Tie a large and a small cookie together with some ribbon and serve.

Advance preparation: make the dough up to 2 days before, cover with plastic wrap and chill. Allow the dough to soften for 20 minutes before using. Bake and decorate the cookies 2 days before and store in single layers in airtight boxes.
Freezing: freeze the dough in batches 4 weeks ahead. The baked biscuits can be made and frozen 3 weeks before. Crisp up in the oven at 350°F/180°C/Gas 4 for 3-4 minutes. Cool and decorate up to 2 days ahead. Store as above.

Chocolate cookies with coffee-praline cream

These chocolate and coffee cream cookies, together with the ice-cream filled chocolate cases (page 83), make a perfectly delicious ending to a drinks party. MAKES 10

⅛ (4oz/110g) x Chocolate Cookie Dough Recipe (see left)
Flour, for rolling
3oz/75g dark semi-sweet chocolate
for the praline
1 rounded tblsp almonds, or hazelnuts with skins
1 rounded tblsp sugar
for the coffee cream
4½ tblsp double cream [heavy cream]
1 tsp Camp chicory & coffee essence, or strong cold sweetened coffee
You will also need a 1¾in/4.5cm fluted cutter, a piping bag and a ½in/1cm star nozzle

Roll the dough out to a thickness of ⅛in/3mm on a lightly floured surface. Stamp out 10 cookies and transfer to a baking tray. Chill for 30 minutes.
Heat the oven to 350°F/180°C/Gas 4 and bake the cookies for 8 minutes, or until slightly darker in colour. Lift them onto a wire rack to cool.
Put the nuts and sugar together in a small pan over a low heat, without stirring, until the sugar has melted to a deep golden colour. This will take about 8-10 minutes. Pour onto a lightly greased baking tray to cool.
Break the set praline into pieces before quickly pulsing in a blender 7-8 times until you have fine crumbs. Alternatively, put the praline in a strong plastic bag and crush it with a rolling pin.
Melt the chocolate in a bowl over a pan of simmering water, pour it onto a plastic tray and set aside to cool. When it has set, draw a cheese slicer across the surface to make curls and then chill them.
Whip the cream until it justs holds its shape, stir in the essence or cold coffee, then fold in the praline.
Spoon the flavoured cream into a piping bag, pipe onto the biscuits and decorate with chocolate curls. Serve.

Happy birthday cup cakes

I think these bite-sized orange cup cakes are a fun way to celebrate a birthday, anniversary or festive occasion. Pipe a message on them and decorate however your artistic talents allow. MAKES 48

for the orange cup cakes
3½oz/95g [7 tblsp] unsalted butter, softened + extra for greasing
4oz/110g caster sugar [heaped ½ cup granulated sugar]
Finely grated zest of 1½ medium oranges
1 medium egg
2 tblsp orange juice
5½oz/165g self-raising flour [heaped 1 cup self-rising flour], sifted

for the glacé icing
9oz/250g icing sugar [2 cups confectioners' sugar], sifted
4½ tblsp warm water
1 tblsp orange flower water, or orange juice, strained

for the royal icing
3 large egg whites, lightly whisked
15oz/425g icing sugar [3½ cups confectioners' sugar], sifted
2 different food colourings
You will also need 4 sets of 12 mini muffin tins 1½in/4cm in diameter, 48 small paper cake cases, 2 piping bags, 2 small star nozzles and 1 small plain nozzle

Heat the oven to 350°F/180°C/Gas 4 and line the muffin tins with the paper cases.
Beat the butter, sugar and orange zest together for 2 minutes or until light and creamy. Beat in the egg and orange juice, then fold in the flour.
Divide this mixture between the muffin tins and bake until risen and golden. Lift the cakes out onto a wire rack to cool.

Happy birthday cup cakes

Make the glacé icing by putting the sugar in a bowl and making a well in the centre. Slowly incorporate the water until the icing is very smooth. Mix in the orange flower water or strained orange juice.
Use the glacé icing immediately or a skin will form on it. Spoon the icing onto the cakes and allow it to set for about 1 hour.
Mix the egg whites and sugar together for the royal icing until stiff but pipeable. Divide into thirds and tint one batch with one colour, another batch with another colour and leave the remainder white.

Decorate the edges of the cakes with the white royal icing using a star nozzle. Pipe the message on the cakes with one colour, using the other star nozzle. Use the other coloured icing and the plain nozzle to decorate the rest with hearts and flowers. Let dry for 2 hours before serving.

Vanilla shortbreads with fromage frais & lime curd

These oh-so-pretty scallop-edged shortbreads are good enough to serve on their own but the easy fromage frais and lime curd topping is a nice touch, particularly for celebratory occasions. MAKES 12

for the vanilla shortbreads
2oz/50g [4 tblsp] unsalted butter + extra for greasing
4oz/110g plain flour [¾ cup all-purpose flour], sifted + extra for rolling
1oz/25g [2 tblsp] vanilla sugar
A pinch of salt

for the fromage frais & lime curd topping
2 tblsp fromage frais or blanc, or lightly whipped cream
2 tsp lime or lemon curd
A few shavings of cedro, or candied citrus peel, to decorate
You will also need a 2⅓in/6cm fluted cutter and a ¼in/5mm plain piping nozzle

Blend the butter, flour and salt together in a food processor until it resembles fine breadcrumbs. Mix in the sugar and then turn out onto a lightly floured surface and lightly knead to make a firm dough.
Roll the dough out to a thickness of ¼in/5mm, stamp out 12 discs and lift them onto a lightly greased baking tray.
Use the piping nozzle to stamp out a ring of small circles around the inside edges of the shortbread discs to decorate them. Chill for 30 minutes.
Heat the oven to 350°F/180°C/Gas 4 and bake the shortbreads for 12 minutes or until they are light golden. Transfer them to a wire rack to cool.
Spoon the fromage frais onto the shortbreads and top with a little lime curd. Swirl the two together with a skewer then decorate with the peel and serve.

Advance preparation: make and bake the shortbread up to 4 days before and store in an airtight container. Top them 30 minutes before serving.
Freezing: freeze the baked shortbreads up to 3 weeks before and crisp up in a preheated oven at 350°F/180°C/Gas 4 for 3-4 minutes. Cool before topping.

Scones with cream & jams

Speed from start to finish is essential when making scones to achieve a light texture. If clotted cream and jam are just too rich for your taste, Greek strained yogurt and honey is a more virtuous substitute. MAKES 10

for the scones
4oz/110g self-raising flour [¾ cup self-rising flour], sifted + extra for rolling
1oz/25g [2 tblsp] unsalted butter, diced + extra for greasing
A pinch of salt
1 tblsp caster sugar [granulated sugar]
4 tblsp milk + 1 tblsp lemon juice for souring
1 tblsp milk, for glazing
for the filling
2 tblsp clotted cream, or whipped cream
2 tblsp jam, such as apricot, blackcurrant or raspberry
You will also need a 1⅛in/4cm plain round cutter

Rub the flour, butter and salt together until the mixture resembles fine crumbs. Mix in the sugar then quickly stir in the milk, which has been soured with the lemon juice, to make a soft dough.
Turn the dough out onto a floured surface and knead it very lightly.
Roll the dough out gently to a thickness of ½in/1cm and stamp out the scones. Reroll any trimmings and stamp out, remembering they will not be as light as the first batch, nor will they rise as evenly.
Put onto a greased baking tray and brush the tops with milk. Rest for 5 minutes.
Heat the oven to 425°F/220°C/Gas 7 and bake the scones for 7 minutes or until well risen and golden brown. Remove and cool on a wire rack.
Split the scones, spoon in the cream and jam and serve.

Advance preparation: bake the scones up to 8 hours before and store in an airtight container. Fill 1 hour before serving, cover and keep cool.
Freezing: freeze the baked scones 3 weeks ahead and freshen up in a hot oven set to 350°F/180°C/Gas 4 for 2-3 minutes. Cool, then fill as above.

Tiny Christmas puddings on cinnamon shortbreads

Dramatic, in spite of their diminutive size, these Christmas puddings are always greeted with childish delight. Serve these and the Christmas dinner tartlets together at a festive cocktail party. MAKES 10

½ x Vanilla Shortbread Recipe (left) made with ½ tsp ground cinnamon
Butter, for greasing
Flour, for dusting
4oz/110g Christmas or plum pudding
1oz/25g ready-made white marzipan
1oz/25g ready-made white icing
Red & green food colouring
Icing sugar [confectioners' sugar], for dusting
1 tsp apricot jam

You will also need a 1½in/4cm and a 1in/2.5cm fluted round cutter, and a tiny holly leaf cutter

Follow the basic vanilla shortbread recipe as given left, adding the ground cinnamon to the sifted flour.

Heat the oven to 350°F/180°C/Gas 4. Roll the dough out to a thickness of ¼in/5mm on a lightly floured surface, then stamp out 10 discs and lift them onto a lightly greased baking tray.

Bake the shortbreads in the oven for 12 minutes or until light golden. Transfer them to a wire rack to cool.

Divide the Christmas or plum pudding into 10 pieces and roll each into a ball.

Break off a third of the marzipan and add a few drops of red colouring to it.

Add green colouring to the remaining marzipan and knead both batches well to incorporate the colours.

Roll out the green marzipan on a surface lightly dusted with icing sugar and stamp out 20 holly leaves using the holly cutter.

Make 30 tiny berries from the red marzipan, giving 3 berries per pudding.

Roll the white icing out on a surface lightly dusted with icing sugar and, using the 1in/2.5cm fluted cutter, stamp out 10 small circles of icing.

Cover the top of each Christmas pudding ball with a small fluted circle of icing.

Moisten a fine pastry brush, dampen the icing leaves and berries and stick them on top of the fluted circles.

Set the oven to 375°F/190°C/Gas 5. Lift the decorated puddings onto the cinnamon shortbreads and transfer them to a baking sheet. Cover loosely with foil.

Warm the puddings though in the oven for 12-15 minutes, or until hot. Serve.

Advance preparation: bake the cinnamon shortbreads and roll and decorate the Christmas puddings up to 4 days before and store separately in airtight containers.

Freezing: freeze the baked shortbreads up to 3 weeks ahead and crisp up in a preheated oven at 350°F/180°C/Gas 4 for 2-3 minutes. Cool before use.

Tiny Christmas puddings on cinnamon shortbreads

the menu

Lacquered sesame nuts

Rice crackers with crispy vegetables

Toasted brioche with crème fraîche & caviar

Crispy duck pancakes

Salmon caviar blinis

Bay scallops with Thai dipping sauce

Passionfruit & papaya won-tons

Chocolate cups with ice-cream

New Orleans coffee with chocolate spoons

Gold vodka

cocktails

Clockwise from top right:
*a friendly bowl of mixed nuts
(and why not?) glazed with
sesame seeds; tropical fruit and
soft cheese top a crisply fried
won-ton wrapper; lay out the
brioche, crème fraîche and caviar
and let guests help themselves;
buy a jar of pickled veg and pile
it on to rice crackers for a no-
effort canapé with class; chives
tie crispy duck pancakes into a
roll for easy, elegant eating.*

Above left: *a classic combination of vodka, glistening salmon roe, sour cream and blinis. Make it even more special by adding edible gold leaf to the drink.* Above right: *we've come a long way from diced cheese and cocktail onions on toothpicks. Here, seared scallops, fresh herbs and pickled ginger get the sharp treatment.* Left: *spoons dipped into chocolate are an elegant touch. Use them to stir spiced coffee and then say goodnight.*

Left: *bubbly red shiraz adds sparkle and sophistication to a party, and all you have to do is chill the bottle then open and pour.* Below: *another easy treat. Bite-sized dark chocolate cups are filled with a selection of ice-creams scooped with a melon baller. Simply buy the chocolate cups and some good quality ices, combine them two days before the party and serve straight from the freezer.*

fork

Stand up and be contented. This chapter is full of **tasty ideas** for parties where you want to **make a meal** of it. Knives get the **chop** when guests are not at table, so food has to sit easily on the fork and **stay there**, all the way into the mouth. You will want to offer choice along with the **heartwarming hospitality**, so **here is the scoop** on forkable meat, chicken and fish dishes, plenty of pasta, **lots of rice**. There are terrific tarts, **salads** of all kinds, beans too. Desserts range from **unctuous** syllabubs to peachy-keen baked fruits, exotic ices and **very necessary chocolate cake**. The feature pages in this section focus on the season of good cheer and **freewheeling** forky occasions such as **brunches** and picnics (there are chopsticks in those pictures, but you **get the idea**). Fill 'em up with dishes laid out on a **table** for guests to help themselves, or **serve** the food from a tray. A **buffet** by any other name would taste as sweet, but you can always skip the party and **eat this food** in front of the telly. **Bliss**.

FOOD

Roast beef salad

Most of the preparation for this rustic salad can be done well ahead but don't slice the beef until just before serving. SERVES 10

5 large red sweet peppers
4 red onions, sliced into ½in/1cm rounds
1½ tblsp olive oil
2½lb/1.15kg beef fillet [tenderloin]
1 tsp black peppercorns, lightly crushed
2 tblsp vegetable oil
10floz/275ml soured cream
3 tblsp creamed horseradish
3 heads radicchio, torn into large pieces
12oz/350g [about 1½ cups] drained
  bottled char-grilled artichokes in oil
Salt & freshly ground black pepper

Grill [broil] the peppers until the skins are blackened. Place in a bowl, cover with plastic wrap and stand for 10 minutes.
Peel and seed the peppers and set the flesh aside to cool before chilling.
Put the onions in a single layer on a baking sheet, drizzle with olive oil and season. Grill [broil] for about 6 minutes on one side until they are slightly charred. Lift onto a plate to cool. Cover and chill.
Roll the beef in the crushed peppercorns.
Heat the vegetable oil in a roasting pan in an oven set to 425°F/220°C/Gas 7 for 5 minutes or until very hot. Add the beef, sear it well on all sides, then roast for 15-20 minutes for rare, or 25-30 minutes for medium. Cool, cover and chill.
Cut the beef into ¼in/5mm slices. Mix the soured cream and horseradish together to make a dressing then season to taste. Cut the grilled peppers into wide strips.
Arrange the radicchio, peppers, onion, beef and artichokes on a dish. Spoon over some of the dressing and serve.

Advance preparation: grill the peppers up to 3 days ahead, the beef up to 2 days ahead; grill the onions and make the dressing up to 1 day ahead, cover and chill. Assemble 1 hour before, cover and keep cool; dress just before serving.
Freezing: not suitable.

Sticky gingered beef

Tossing the beef in sugar gives it a caramel taste and lovely rich colour. SERVES 10

5 spring onions [scallions], halved
  crossways
2½lb/1.15kg lean beef, cut into strips
4 tblsp sugar
1½lb/700g [3¾ cups] basmati rice
18-20 saffron threads
1 tblsp boiling water
4 tblsp toasted sesame oil
for the sauce
6floz/175ml white wine vinegar
10floz/275ml hoisin sauce
1 tblsp Worcestershire sauce
A few drops of Tabasco sauce
4 small pieces stem ginger, finely
  chopped
Salt & freshly ground black pepper

Cut the spring onions into long thin strips and put them into a bowl of iced water for about 20 minutes to crisp and curl.
Coat the beef with the sugar.
Wash the rice in several changes of water and drain well.
Mix the saffron with the boiling water and leave to stand for 10 minutes.
Boil the rice and saffron in a large pan of salted water for 8-10 minutes or until the rice is soft outside but firm inside. Drain, cover with foil and keep warm.
Heat some of the sesame oil in a wok or heavy-based frying pan. Stir-fry the beef in batches for 3-5 minutes until browned. Transfer each cooked batch to a plate.
Add the vinegar to the wok and simmer over a high heat until it has reduced to a volume of around 4 tablespoons.
Lower the heat to medium and add the hoisin, Worcestershire and Tabasco sauces and the chopped ginger. Season. When the sauce starts to bubble, add the beef and heat through for 2-3 minutes.
Drain and dry the spring onions.
Spoon the hot rice and beef into separate serving dishes. Garnish the beef with the spring onions and serve.

Advance preparation: chop the ginger up to 2 days before, cover and keep cool. Cut the spring onions, place in iced water,

cover and chill; slice the beef, cover and chill up to 1 day ahead.
Freezing: not suitable.

Saffron lamb tagine

Dates, prunes and apricots can be used instead of raisins or cranberries. SERVES 10

18-20 saffron threads
1 tblsp boiling water
5lb/2.25kg lamb fillet [boneless neck of
  lamb], cut into large dice
4 tblsp vegetable oil
1lb/450g cippolini, button or pearl onions
1 large clove garlic, crushed
1 tsp ground ginger
A large pinch of cayenne pepper
½ tsp cinnamon
1lb/450g canned chopped tomatoes
2 pints/1.2 litres [5 cups] chicken stock
1oz/25g [2½ tblsp] raisins
3oz/75g [½ cup] unskinned almonds
1oz/25g [2 tblsp] butter
1oz/25g [3 tblsp] pistachios, peeled
1oz/25g [3 tblsp] dried cranberries

Heat the oven to 375°F/190°C/Gas 5. Mix the saffron with the boiling water and leave to stand for 10 minutes.
Fry the lamb in batches in hot oil over a high heat for 2-3 minutes to brown it on all sides. Remove with a slotted spoon and transfer to an ovenproof dish.
Pour off all but 1 tablespoon of the oil from the pan, lower the heat and cook the onions in it for 4-5 minutes until golden.
Stir in the garlic, spices and saffron liquid and cook for 1 minute. Add the tomatoes, stock and raisins, bring to the boil, season well. Stir into the lamb, cover and cook in the oven for 1½ hours, or until tender.
Sauté the almonds in hot butter for 1-2 minutes, then add the pistachios, cranberries and a large pinch of salt. Scatter over the lamb tagine and serve.

Advance preparation: make up to 3 days ahead, cover and cool. Reheat in a preheated oven at 375°F/190°C/Gas 5 for 45-60 minutes, until piping hot.
Freezing: freeze the cooked tagine up to 4 weeks before and reheat as above.

Chicken tonnato salad

Delicious though tuna fish sauce is with that classic Italian dish of vitello tonnato, it's also pretty wonderful with chicken. SERVES 10

10 x 6oz/175g boneless chicken breasts, skinned
Oil, for greasing
10oz/275g French beans [haricot verts]
5oz/150g [1 cup] black olives
20 anchovies stuffed with capers
Salt & freshly ground black pepper
for the tuna sauce
4 rounded tblsp mayonnaise
3oz/75g canned tuna in oil + 2 tblsp of the oil
1 rounded tblsp capers
1 tblsp lemon juice

Season and cook the chicken on a lightly oiled ridged grill-pan for 8-10 minutes, turning once, until cooked through. Remove, cool and slice each chicken breast into 6 pieces.
Cook the beans in boiling salted water for 3-5 minutes or until tender but still with some bite. Drain in a colander, then refresh in cold water until stone cold to retain the colour.
Dry the beans on paper towels, then cut them in half lengthways.

Put the mayonnaise in a food processor and blend with the tuna, oil, capers, lemon juice and pepper until smooth.
Arrange the chicken on a serving dish and drizzle over the tuna sauce. Place the beans, olives and the stuffed anchovies on top and serve.

Advance preparation: make the sauce up to 2 days before; grill the chicken and cook the beans up to 1 day ahead, cover and chill. Assemble up to 1 hour before, cover and chill.
Freezing: not suitable.

Vietnamese chicken salad

This is a sensational salad – light, pretty and with a distinctive, fresh tasting sauce. The sauce, nuoc cham, is Vietnam's equivalent to the soy sauce of China and Japan, in that it's liberally used in cooking and as an accompaniment to food. SERVES 10

10 x 6oz/175g boneless chicken breasts, skinned
8floz/225ml water
4 tblsp white wine
3 tblsp olive oil
1 bay leaf
8 black peppercorns

11oz/300g carrot
11oz/300g cucumber
11oz/300g white radish (daikon or mooli)
5oz/150g [1½ cups] beansprouts
4oz/110g Chinese leaves [1½ cups Napa Valley cabbage], cut into ⅓in/1cm wide strips
2oz/50g mixed Asian salad leaves, such as mizuna & tat soi
1oz/25g [½ cup] mint leaves
1oz/25g coriander leaves [½ cup cilantro leaves]
Salt
for the nuoc cham dressing
4 tblsp lime juice
3 tblsp Thai fish sauce
3 tblsp rice vinegar
3 tblsp vegetable oil
2 tblsp palm sugar, or dark brown sugar
1 medium-sized hot red chilli, seeded & finely chopped
2 medium cloves garlic, crushed

Combine all the dressing ingredients and leave for 30 minutes.
Heat the oven to 375°F/190°C/Gas 5. Put the chicken with the water, wine, oil, bay leaf, peppercorns and some salt into a roasting pan. Cover with foil and cook in the oven for about 15-20 minutes or until it is cooked through.
Remove the chicken from the oven, drain and cool on paper towels. Slice each breast into 8 pieces.
Cut the carrots and cucumber into chunky pieces. Shave the radish into very fine ribbons using a vegetable peeler.
Toss the chicken, vegetables, salad leaves and herbs together in the dressing, arrange on a platter and serve.

Advance preparation: make the dressing and cook the chicken up to 2 days before. Prepare the carrots and radish and put into water, and prepare the cucumber up to 1 day ahead, cover and chill. Assemble up to 1 hour before, cover and chill.
Freezing: not suitable.

Chicken tonnato salad

right Vietnamese chicken salad

Chicken scaloppine with mozzarella & sage

Chicken layered with mozzarella cheese, paper-thin prosciutto, a sliver of pungent garlic and quickly fried in olive oil, is my idea of food heaven. SERVES 10

10 x 6oz/175g boneless chicken breasts, each cut into 4
10 slices prosciutto di Parma, halved widthways
4 balls mozzarella, each sliced into 5
4 cloves garlic, each sliced into 5
20 sage leaves
6floz/175ml olive oil
1¼lb/570g red cherry tomatoes
1¼lb/570g yellow cherry tomatoes
10floz/275ml white wine
15floz/425ml chicken stock
Salt & freshly ground black pepper

Flatten each piece of chicken between 2 sheets of plastic wrap with a rolling pin, until about double in size and around 2½in/6cm in diameter and ¼in/5mm thick. Season well.

Divide the prosciutto, mozzarella and garlic between 20 of the chicken pieces. Top with the remaining chicken and press a sage leaf on top.

Heat the oven to 375°F/190°C/Gas 5. Put the cherry tomatoes into a roasting pan with 2 tablespoons of the olive oil, season and roast for 10 minutes.

Add some of the remaining oil to a large pan and fry the chicken in batches, leaf side down first, over a medium heat, for 3 minutes each side. Remove the chicken, cover and keep warm while frying the rest.

Pour the wine into the pan and let it simmer for 1 minute before adding the stock and bringing it to the boil. Cook until reduced by a third, then season.

Return the scaloppini to the pan, lower the heat to a simmer and heat through for 2 minutes. Serve, sage leaves uppermost, with the roasted tomatoes.

Advance preparation: prepare the chicken to the point of cooking up to 1 day before, cover and chill. Cook the chicken and tomatoes to order.
Freezing: not suitable.

Butter chicken masala

A wonderfully hot but beautifully creamy chicken dish. If you can't stand hot food, halve, or even quarter, the amount of chilli powder used. Serve the curry with lots of plain boiled basmati rice and a glass of the Coconut Cooler (page 152). Do not be deterred by the long list of ingredients in this recipe as most of them are commonly used store cupboard spices. SERVES 10

6lb/2.7kg boned, skinned chicken
for the marinade
7floz/200ml plain yogurt
1 tblsp olive oil
2 tblsp lemon juice
1 tsp turmeric
2 tsp garam masala
1 tblsp hot chilli powder
2 tsp ground cumin
2 tsp finely grated ginger

2 large cloves garlic, crushed
2 tsp salt
for the sauce
4oz/110g [¾ cup] cashew nuts
1 large onion, finely chopped
4 tblsp olive oil
1 medium clove garlic, crushed
1 tblsp finely grated ginger
10floz/275ml water
5oz/150g [⅔ cup] tomato paste

2 tblsp clear honey
4 tblsp double cream [heavy cream]
1 bay leaf
5 curry leaves + extra for garnishing
A large pinch of fenugreek
A large pinch of ground cardamom
2 tsp garam masala
1oz/25g [2 tblsp] butter
1 tblsp cardamom pods
Salt

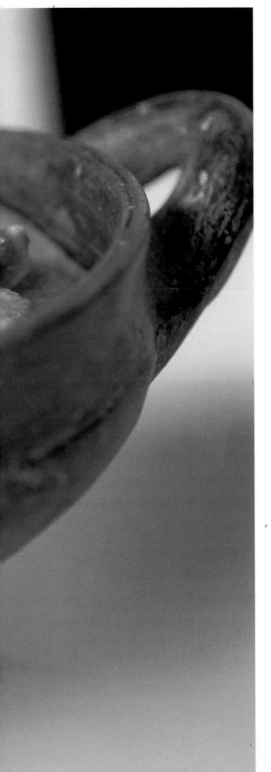

Cut the chicken into large pieces.
Mix all the marinade ingredients together, coat the chicken with this mixture, cover and marinate for 8 hours in the fridge.
Heat the oven to 400°F/200°C/Gas 6. Divide the marinated chicken between 2 roasting pans and cook in the hot oven for 15 minutes.
Blend half the cashew nuts in a food processor for 1 minute to make a paste.
Fry the onion in oil in a large pan over a medium heat for about 5-7 minutes, or until soft and golden brown. Add the garlic and ginger and cook for 1 minute.
Stir in the cashew paste, water, tomato paste, honey, cream, bay leaf, the 5 curry leaves, fenugreek, ground cardamom and garam masala. Mix well, bring to the boil, lower the heat and simmer for 10 minutes until the sauce has thickened to a creamy, coating consistency.
Sauté the cardamom pods and remaining cashew nuts quickly in the butter for 1-2 minutes.
Transfer the cooked chicken from the oven to the pan of sauce and simmer for 10 minutes, ensuring each piece of chicken is well coated.
Spoon the mixture into a serving dish, scatter over the sautéed cashews and cardamom and garnish with the remaining curry leaves. Serve hot.

Advance preparation: make the sauce up to 4 days before; cook the chicken in the sauce up to 2 days before, cover and chill. Reheat in a preheated oven at 375°F/190°C/Gas 5 for 30-40 minutes, until piping hot.
Freezing: freeze the marinated chicken and the sauce separately up to 4 weeks before. Freeze the cooked chicken in the sauce up to 3 weeks before and reheat as above.

left Butter chicken masala

Red duck curry

It should take you about 45 minutes from start to finish to make this fragrant duck curry from South-East Asia. If you want to bulk it up a bit with some vegetables, sautéed pea aubergines [eggplants] and Thai shallots would do the job nicely. Plain boiled jasmine rice is the best accompaniment. SERVES 10

14oz/400g [2⅓ cups] jasmine rice
10 x 8oz/225g duck breasts
4 tblsp Thai red curry paste
2 tblsp lemon grass paste, or 2 sticks
  lemon grass, finely chopped
8 kaffir lime leaves + extra for garnishing
1 large hot red chilli, split & seeded
  + extra whole chillies for garnishing
10floz/275ml coconut milk
10floz/275ml duck or chicken stock
Salt & freshly ground black pepper

Wash the rice in several changes of cold water and drain well.
Remove the skin and fat from the duck and put them into a large pan. Cook over a moderate heat to melt the fat. Reserve 3 tablespoons of this fat in the pan.
Cook the rice in a large pan of boiling, unsalted water for 8 minutes. Lower the heat and cook for a further 3 minutes until the rice is no longer chalky in the centre. Drain, cover and keep warm.
Slice each duck breast into 8 pieces and stir-fry them in the duck fat in batches, over a high heat, for about 3 minutes per batch. Return all the meat to the pan.
Add the curry paste, lemon grass, lime leaves and chilli to the pan and cook for 1 minute over a medium heat. Stir in the coconut milk and stock. Cover, reduce the heat to low and simmer for 10 minutes, or until the duck is tender.
Garnish the curry with the extra lime leaves and chillies and serve with the boiled jasmine rice.

Advance preparation: make the curry up to 8 hours ahead, cover and chill. Reheat gently for about 10 minutes or until hot. Cook the rice up to 1 hour ahead, cover with foil and keep warm in an oven set to 275°F/140°C/Gas 1.
Freezing: not suitable.

Seared salmon, asparagus & potato salad

A very English salad that is best made with new season's salmon, potatoes and asparagus. Ideally, serve it slightly warm, but if that's not possible, serve it cold and make sure that you take it out of the fridge a good half an hour beforehand. Finish the meal with a bowl of jewel-bright Red Berry Kissel (page 132) and some clotted cream. SERVES 10

2¼lb/1kg small new waxy potaoes, unpeeled
1lb10oz/750g salmon fillet, skinned
1 tblsp olive oil + extra for greasing
2 tsp Maldon or flaked sea salt
½ tsp paprika
12oz/350g asparagus, each spear cut diagonally into 3
1 rounded tblsp chervil leaves
1 rounded tblsp mint leaves
1 rounded tblsp basil leaves
Salt & freshly ground black pepper
for the mustard dressing
1 tblsp sweet mustard
2 tblsp olive oil
4 tblsp lemon juice
1½ tsp sugar

Whisk all the dressing ingredients together and season to taste.
Cook the potatoes in boiling salted water for 10-12 minutes or until tender.

Drain, cool a little, cut in half then pour over half the mustard dressing and toss well. The potatoes will absorb more flavour if you do this while they are hot.
Rub the salmon on both sides, first with the oil and then with a mixture of the salt and paprika.
Sear the fish on a very hot, oiled, ridged cast-iron grill-pan on either side, for 8-10 minutes in total, until crisp and golden on the outside and still slightly pink on the middle. Transfer to a tray to cool and break into neat, forkable pieces.
Boil the asparagus for about 3 minutes in a pan of salted water until al dente. Drain in a colander under running cold water to preserve the colour then dry on paper towels. Alternatively, cook the spears on the grill-pan for 4-5 minutes.
Arrange the potatoes, salmon and asparagus in a dish. Drizzle over the remaining dressing and scatter over a mixture of the fresh herbs. Serve.

Advance preparation: make the dressing up to 2 days before; cook the salmon, potatoes and asparagus up to 1 day ahead, cover and chill. Assemble up to 4 hours before, except for the herbs, cover and chill. Remove from the fridge 30 minutes before serving and scatter over the herbs.
Freezing: not suitable.

Courgette & seafood salad

Tossed in a refreshing lemon olive oil dressing, this salad of scallops, prawns, squid, paper-thin raw courgettes and a few leaves, is ideal served as part of a buffet, or on its own. Squid goes through three stages of cooking – tender, tough, tender. To get the best results, it needs to be cooked briefly for 1 or 2 minutes, or for a long time, as anything in-between makes it rubbery. SERVES 10

20 small scallops
4floz/120ml lemon olive oil, or extra virgin olive oil
1lb/450g squid, cut into fine rings
1 medium clove garlic, crushed
2 tblsp lemon juice
20 cooked peeled large prawns or shrimps
3oz/75g [¾ cup] baby spinach
5oz/150g baby courgettes [heaped 1 cup zucchini], very finely sliced
2 rounded tblsp chervil leaves
Salt & freshly ground black pepper

Sauté the scallops in batches in 2 tablespoons of the oil over a high heat for 1-2 minutes, or until just cooked. Remove from the pan and set aside.
Cook the squid and garlic in batches in another 2 tablespoons of the oil, also over a high temperature, very briefly for 1-2 minutes, until opaque and tender.
Leave the scallops and the squid to cool.
Whisk the remaining oil with the lemon juice and some seasoning.
Put all the salad ingredients, except for the chervil, in a bowl and lightly toss in the lemon dressing. Scatter over the chervil leaves and serve.

Advance preparation: cook the scallops and squid; crush the garlic; slice the courgettes and make the lemon dressing up to 6 hours before, cover and chill. Assemble up to 30 minutes ahead.
Freezing: not suitable.

Seared salmon, asparagus & potato salad

right Courgette & seafood salad

Thai mussels

These steamed mussels, in a refreshing aromatic Thai broth, give their French counterpart, moules marinière, a good run for their money. SERVES 10

6 stalks lemon grass
4 tomatoes
1 pint/570ml [2½ cups] water
6 cloves garlic, crushed
11oz/300g Thai red shallots, halved
4in/10cm piece galangal, or root ginger, sliced
10lbs/4.5kg mussels
1 tsp hot red chilli flakes
2 large fresh hot green chillies, split & seeded
4 tblsp Thai fish sauce
2 tblsp palm sugar, or dark brown sugar

Pound the lemon grass with a pestle or mallet to crush.

Put the tomatoes into a bowl, pour over boiling water to cover and leave for about 10 seconds. Plunge them into cold water, peel off the skin, then quarter the tomatoes and remove and discard the seeds. Roughly chop the tomato flesh.

Divide the measured water, lemon grass, garlic, shallots and galangal between 2 large pans. Bring to the boil and then divide the tomatoes, chilli flakes, fresh chillies, fish sauce, sugar and mussels between these pans.

Cover and cook them at maximum heat for 4-5 minutes, until all the mussels have opened. Discard any which have not, along with the lemon grass stalks.

Transfer the mussels and vegetable broth to bowls and serve.

Advance preparation: prepare the tomatoes up to 4 hours before, cover and chill. Cook the mussels to order.
Freezing: not suitable.

left Thai mussels

Bruschetta with red mullet, fried crumbs & capers

Crisp bruschetta oozing with olive oil, draped with red mullet fillets and scattered with fried crumbs make a tasty first course, or main course. Some rocket [arugula] leaves would be an attractive and delicious accompaniment. SERVES 10

10 x 3oz/75g red mullet fillets
10floz/275ml white wine
2 tsp hot red chilli flakes
2 tsp Maldon or flaked sea salt
5oz/150g [2½ cups] coarse breadcrumbs
4 tblsp olive oil
2 rounded tblsp capers preserved in balsamic vinegar
10 x ½in/1cm slices ciabatta bread
10 tblsp lemon olive oil or extra virgin olive oil
1 rounded tblsp chopped parsley
5 small lemons, halved lengthways

Heat the oven to 375°F/190°C/Gas 5. Put the red mullet skin-side up in a roasting pan with the white wine. Sprinkle over the chilli flakes and salt.

Roast in the oven for 8-10 minutes until cooked. Lift onto paper towels to drain.

Fry the breadcrumbs in 2 tablespoons of the olive oil over a medium heat, stirring constantly, for 2-3 minutes until crisp and golden. Add the capers during the last minute of frying. Keep warm.

Grill the ciabatta bread on both sides on a very hot ridged cast-iron grill-pan until crisp, or toast under a preheated grill [broiler]. Drizzle the bread with the remaining 2 tablespoons of olive oil.

Place a roasted mullet fillet on top of each slice of toasted bread, then spoon over the fried crumbs and capers.

Drizzle with the lemon olive oil or extra virgin oil and garnish with the chopped parsley and a lemon half. Serve the bruschetta warm to hot.

Advance preparation: fry the crumbs up to 2 days ahead and cover. Chop the parsley up to 1 day before, cover and chill. Reheat the crumbs in a pan with the capers for 1 minute. Cook the mullet and bruschetta to order.
Freezing: freeze the fried crumbs up to 4 weeks in advance.

Bruschetta with red mullet, fried crumbs & capers

the menu

Grissini & rouille dip

Bacon & egg linguine

Green salad

Red berry kissel with biscotti & vanilla cream

Cheese & fresh figs

Oyster shooters

Lime, orange & lemon citrus pressé

brunch

Clockwise from top right:
*bacon and eggs are perfect
morning food and delicious mixed
with pasta and herbs; a luscious
fruity conclusion – Red Berry
Kissel can be used in myriad
ways but here it is simply served
with flavoured cream; brunch is
casual so guests will be happy to
see you preparing the food and
may even be keen to help;
indispensable Green Salad with
balsamic dressing.*

Below: *serve the Lime, Orange & Lemon Citrus Pressé in colourful tumblers to complement the flavours of the drink and garnish with contrasting twists of peel.* Right: *a whole fine cheese served with baguette or rustic sourdough, mounds of crunchy walnuts still in their shells and fresh summery figs. Shopping is the only preparation required and guests can serve themselves.*

Top: *these grissini are made
from a simple bread recipe then
rolled with flavourings such as
olives, red chilli, sea salt and
herbs before baking. Serve them
with a spicy rouille for dipping,
made by your own hand or
bought from a good store if time
is tight. Left: Oyster Shooters
are a glamorous alternative to
the traditional brunch-time
Bloody Mary and an excellent
wake-up call for any guests who
are still feeling sleepy.*

·10 am·

Scrambled eggs with garlic & thyme

These creamy scrambled eggs are flavoured with garlic and thyme and then piled back in their shells. Suitable for brunches, lunches and suppers, serve them with some home-made grissini 'soldiers' to dip. SERVES 10

14 large eggs
3 large cloves garlic, cut into 20 slices
2 tsp olive oil
3oz/75g [6 tblsp] unsalted butter
4 tblsp double cream [heavy cream]
10 sprigs thyme
1 x Grissini Recipe (page 37)
Salt & freshly ground black pepper

Cut the tops off the eggs with a serrated knife and pour the yolks and whites into a bowl. Wash and dry 10 of the best egg shells and put them into egg cups.
Fry the garlic in oil over a medium heat for 5-7 minutes until crisp and golden. Drain on paper towels.
Pass the eggs through a sieve to remove the stringy bits.
Melt the butter in a small, heavy pan over a very low heat, add the eggs and stir constantly, for about 3-5 minutes, until they are creamy with light curds and just hold their shape.
Remove from the heat, stir in the cream and seasoning. Transfer to a bowl, otherwise the eggs will carry on cooking.
Spoon the scrambled eggs into the egg shells, top with the garlic and thyme and serve with the grissini.

Advance preparation: prepare the egg shells and roast the garlic up to 1 day before, cover.
Freezing: not suitable.

Fried Mexican eggs with chorizo & spicy salsa

Fried Mexican eggs with chorizo & spicy salsa

These Mexican eggs, perfect for brunches, call out to be served with an icy-cold glass of beer. SERVES 10

10 x ½in/1cm slices bread
9oz/250g Spanish chorizo, sliced into 30
Vegetable oil, for frying
10 medium eggs
Salt & freshly ground black pepper
for the spicy salsa
5 plum or salad tomatoes
5 tblsp tomato passata [tomato purée]
3 tblsp chopped coriander [cilantro]
2 large hot red chillies, seeded & roughly chopped
2 tblsp olive oil
1 medium clove garlic, crushed
You will also need a 3in/7.5cm round cutter

Stamp out discs from the centre of each slice of bread using the cutter.
Put the tomatoes into a bowl, pour over boiling water to cover and leave for about 10 seconds. Plunge them into cold water, peel, quarter and discard the seeds.
Chop the tomato flesh roughly and mix it with the passata, chilli and coriander to make the salsa.

Warm the olive oil over a low heat, add the garlic, fry for 1 minute and then add the tomato mixture and heat until the salsa is hot, for about 5 minutes. Season.
Dry-fry the chorizo in a very hot frying pan for 30 seconds on either side, until heated through. Cover and keep warm at the side of the stove.
Heat the vegetable oil in a large frying pan, fry the bread in batches over a medium heat on one side only until crisp.
Turn the bread over and put it back into the pan, again in batches.
Crack an egg into the middle of each piece of bread and fry for 2-3 minutes, spooning hot oil over the top of the eggs to cook them.
Season the eggs, transfer to plates, spoon over the salsa and arrange a few slices of chorizo on the side. Serve.

Advance preparation: stamp the bread out, prepare the salsa up the point of cooking and slice the chorizo up to 1 day before, cover and chill. Fry the chorizo, bread and eggs to order. Heat the salsa as above.
Freezing: not suitable.

left Scrambled eggs with garlic & thyme

Gruyère, artichoke & mortadella tart

This mix of char-grilled artichokes, sautéed mortadella and gruyère in a rosemary custard, makes a distinctive, rustic and well-flavoured tart. SERVES 10

1 x Savoury Shortcrust Pastry Recipe
    (page 56)
Flour, for rolling
for the filling
10oz/275g mortadella, cut into
    1in/2.5cm pieces
1 tblsp olive oil
10oz/275g [1¼ cups] drained bottled
    char-grilled artichokes in oil, halved
6oz/175g [1½ cups] gruyère, grated
10floz/275ml double cream [heavy cream]
3 large eggs

1 large egg yolk
1 tblsp finely chopped rosemary
Salt & freshly ground black pepper
*You will also need a 10in/25.5cm
shallow loose-bottomed fluted tart tin,
baking parchment and baking beans.*

Roll the chilled pastry thinly on a lightly floured surface to a circle 2in/5cm larger than the tin. Wrap the pastry around the rolling pin and let it unroll over the tin, pressing it down into the bottom and up the sides. Roll the pin over the top of the tin to trim away any excess pastry and give a clean edge. Lightly prick the base with a fork and chill for 30 minutes.
Fry the mortadella in hot oil over a medium heat for 4-5 minutes or until evenly browned. Drain on paper towels.

Heat the oven to 400°F/200°C/Gas 6.
Line the tart with baking parchment and baking beans and then bake the pastry for 15 minutes. Remove the parchment and beans and bake for a further 5 minutes until golden. Cool a little.
Arrange the mortadella, artichokes and cheese on the bottom of the tart case.
Whisk together the cream, eggs, yolk, rosemary and seasoning. Pour into the tart and bake in the hot oven for 20 minutes, or until the custard has set.
Cool the tart for 10 minutes before removing it from the tin to a serving dish. Serve hot or cold.

Advance preparation: bake the tart case, fry the mortadella and make the custard up to 1 day before; store the tart case in an airtight container; cover and chill the mortadella and custard. Bake to order if serving hot, allowing an extra 5 minutes cooking time. If serving cold, bake up to 12 hours ahead, cover and chill. Remove from the fridge 1 hour before serving.
Freezing: the tart can be frozen unbaked in its tin for up to 1 week and baked straight from the freezer. Freeze it baked up to 3 weeks ahead.

Tomato & pesto galette

Stunningly easy to make, particularly if you choose to buy both the pastry and the pesto, this galette is a good do-ahead recipe when time is short. Substitute tapenade for pesto if you prefer. Serve at brunches or suppers, with the Rocket, French Bean, Red Onion & Croûton Salad (page 128). SERVES 10

2½lb/1.15kg puff pastry
Flour, for dusting
Butter, for greasing
5 x Chunky Pesto Recipe (page 43), or
    15oz/425g [1⅔ cups] ready-made pesto
10 plum tomatoes, thinly sliced
3 tblsp olive oil
10 basil sprigs
Salt & freshly ground black pepper

Roll the pastry out on a lightly floured surface to ⅛in/2mm thick. Cut out

Gruyere, artichoke & mortadella tart

10 x 6½in/16cm circles using a small plate as a template. Lift these discs onto 4 lightly greased baking trays, prick with a fork and chill for 30 minutes.

Heat the oven to 400°F/200°C/Gas 6. Bake the pastries in batches for 8-10 minutes until golden. Swap the trays over in the oven halfway through cooking.

Divide the pesto between the pastry galettes, spreading it to the edges. Arrange the tomatoes on top, drizzle with the oil and season.

Grill under a hot grill [broiler] for 1-2 minutes until the tomatoes have softened a little and the pastry is warmed through. Garnish with the basil and serve.

Advance preparation: bake the pastries up to 1 day before and store in an airtight container. Assemble up to 2 hours before and grill to order, allowing an extra 2 minutes for grilling.
Freezing: the baked pastries can be frozen up to 3 weeks ahead. Defrost and grill for an extra 2 minutes.

Polenta, taleggio & wild mushrooms

Polenta taragna is a mixture of polenta and buckwheat flour with a speckled appearance. Adding masses of taleggio and butter makes it very creamy and rich, whilst the garlicky mushrooms improve it some more! This is a wintry, stick-to-the-ribs dish. SERVES 10

for the polenta
4 pints/2.25 litres [10 cups] water
2 tsp salt
1lb/450g [4 cups] polenta taragna, or coarse polenta
7oz/200g [14 tblsp] butter
1lb/450g taleggio cheese, peeled and diced
Freshly ground black pepper
for the wild mushrooms
1lb10oz/750g mixed wild mushrooms, such as black trumpet, girolles, mousserons & pied de moutons
2 large cloves garlic, crushed
4 tblsp olive oil
2oz/50g [4 tblsp] butter
Salt & freshly ground black pepper

Tomato & pesto galette

Bring the water and salt to the boil in a large pan, reduce the heat to a simmer and very slowly pour in the polenta, whisking all the time to prevent lumps.

Mix in half the butter and continue to cook the polenta over a low heat, stirring constantly with a wooden spoon for about 20-25 minutes. The polenta is ready when it is smooth, thick and comes away from the side of the pan.

Sauté the mushrooms and garlic in the oil and butter, in batches, over a high heat for 4-5 minutes or until cooked. Season thoroughly.

Remove the polenta from the heat, stir in the cheese, the rest of the butter and the pepper. Mix well and transfer to a serving dish. Spoon over the cooked mushrooms and any juices. Serve.

Advance preparation: sauté the mushrooms up to 2 hours before and cover. Quickly sauté for 3-4 minutes to reheat. Make the polenta to order.
Freezing: not suitable.

Taboulleh primavera

Serve this taboulleh as a light first course or as an accompaniment to the Courgette & Seafood Salad (page 100). It also makes a good canapé filling when served in hollowed out cucumber cups, but you will need to cut the vegetables smaller. SERVES 10

7½oz/210g [1⅓ cups] cracked wheat
13½floz/385ml boiling water
grated zest & juice of 3 lemons
4½ tblsp olive oil
2½lb/1.15kg broad beans [fava beans], shelled to yield about 8oz/225g
14oz/400g thin asparagus
3oz/75g [¾ cup] sprouting beans
4oz/110g spring onions [1 cup scallions], thinly sliced

2 rounded tblsp mint leaves
1 rounded tblsp chervil sprigs
Salt & freshly ground black pepper

Put the cracked wheat in a bowl with the boiling water, lemon juice and oil. Mix well, cover and leave for 1 hour or until the grains soak up all the liquid.

Cook the broad beans and asparagus separately in pans of boiling salted water for 3 minutes.

Drain and refresh the broad beans and asparagus under running cold water until cold to stop the cooking process and preserve the colour. Dry on paper towels.

Cut the asparagus lengthways in half and then diagonally in half again. Peel and discard the outer skins of the broad beans.

Season the cracked wheat with salt and pepper, then add all the vegetables, plus most of the lemon zest, mint leaves and chervil, and toss gently.

Transfer the mixture to a salad bowl, scatter over the remaining zest, mint and chervil to garnish and serve.

Advance preparation: cook and refresh the broad beans and asparagus, slice the spring onions, zest and squeeze the lemons up to 1 day ahead, cover and chill. Soak the cracked wheat up to 8 hours before, but you may need to add some extra oil and lemon juice if it becomes too dry. Cover and chill. Assemble up to 1 hour before.
Freezing: not suitable.

Taboulleh primavera

Wild & red Camargue rice salad with blood oranges & grilled red onions

Wild & red Camargue rice salad with blood oranges & grilled red onions

Apart from the interesting mix of flavours and textures in this Mediterranean-inspired salad, the range of red colours, from the bold scarlet radishes to the more muted tones of the grilled red onions, make it a striking dish for a summer buffet table. SERVES 10

for the salad

5oz/150g [scant 1 cup] wild rice
5oz/150g [scant 1 cup] red Camargue rice
3 small red onions, sliced into ½in/5mm rounds
2 tblsp olive oil
5 blood oranges
½ cucumber, cut into irregular chunks
1 head red chicory [Belgian endive]
1 bunch radishes, halved through the stalks
Salt & freshly ground black pepper

for the citrus dressing

3floz/75ml olive oil
1 tblsp white wine vinegar
1 tsp balsamic vinegar
4½ tblsp orange juice
Salt & freshly ground black pepper

Cook the wild rice in a pan of salted boiling water for 25 minutes until al dente. Drain in a colander, refresh under cold water and drain again.

Boil the red rice in another pan of boiling salted water for 20 minutes and drain and refresh as before. Do not cook both varieties of rice together as the red rice will stain the wild rice and you will lose the distinct colour of each.

Heat the grill [broiler] to the highest setting. Put the red onions in a single layer on a baking sheet, drizzle over the olive oil and season.

Grill the onions for about 6 minutes on one side only until they are slightly

charred at the edges. Remove from the heat and lift off onto a plate to cool.

Prepare the blood oranges by cutting a slice from the top and bottom of each with a small sharp knife. Carve away the peel and pith following the curve of the fruit, leaving the flesh exposed. Slice into ¼in/5mm circles, flicking out any seeds.

Trim the base of the chicory to separate all the leaves and then cut each leaf lengthways into ⅛in/3mm wide strips.

Whisk all the ingredients for the dressing together in a small bowl and season.

Toss the wild and red rices together in the dressing and season. Mix in the remaining salad ingredients and serve.

Advance preparation: up to 1 day ahead, cook both lots of rice, grill the onions, slice the oranges, make the dressing, cover and chill. Assemble up to 2 hours before.
Freezing: not suitable.

Persian jewelled rice

Dramatic in its brilliant colours from saffron, barberries and pistachios, this elegant Persian jewelled rice can be served as a main course, or with a simple roast chicken dish. Barberries, once used in cooking in medieval England, are available from Iranian food shops, where they are sold dried and known as zereshk. They have a very tart flavour and need to be de-stemmed and rinsed before use. This dish can also be served cold. SERVES 10

10oz/275g [1½cups] basmati rice
18-20 saffron threads
1 tblsp boiling water
1 rounded tsp cardamom pods
1 rounded tsp coriander seeds
3 tblsp olive oil
1oz/25g [3 tblsp] dried barberries
2oz/50g [heaped ⅓ cup] dried cranberries
4oz/110g [⅔ cup] raisins
2oz/50g [⅔ cup] pistachio nuts, peeled
Salt & freshly ground black pepper

Wash the rice in several changes of cold water and drain well. Mix the saffron with the boiling water and leave to stand for 10 minutes.

Add the rice to a large pan of salted boiling water with the cardamom and coriander. Bring it back to the boil and boil for 8-10 minutes, until the rice is soft on the outside but still firm in the centre. Drain in a colander.

Put the oil in a large pan over a medium heat. Add the barberries, cranberries, raisins and pistachios and sauté for 1 minute to plump up the fruits. Stir in the rice and the saffon liquid, season well and mix until piping hot. Serve.

Advance preparation: only if serving cold, make the jewelled rice up to 1 day before, cover and chill. Do not reheat cooked rice.
Freezing: not suitable.

left Persian jewelled rice

Lemon & beetroot risottos

Not only are these two risottos on a plate striking to look at, they both taste wonderful in their own right. The lemon version partners fish extremely well, whilst the sweet flavour of beetroot is a good accompaniment to game and smoked sausages. Risottos cannot be rushed; you need to stand at the stove stirring and adding hot stock all the time so that the rice slowly absorbs all the liquid. That is the secret of good risotto. SERVES 10

for the beetroot risotto

8oz/225g raw beetroot [beets]
Vegetable oil, for deep-frying
1¼ pints/725ml [3 cups] vegetable or
   chicken stock
2 tblsp olive oil
2oz/50g [4 tblsp] butter
1 medium onion, finely chopped
7oz/200g [scant 1 cup] arborio or
   carnaroli rice
10floz/275ml red wine

for the lemon risotto

2½ pints/1.5 litres [1½ quarts] vegetable
   or chicken stock
2 tblsp olive oil
2oz/50g [4 tblsp] butter
1 medium onion, finely chopped
12oz/350g [1½ cups] arborio or
   carnaroli rice
5floz/150ml white wine
Grated zest & juice of 4 lemons
4 tblsp mascarpone
Salt & freshly ground black pepper
Grated parmesan

Cut 10 thin slices from the beetroot and roughly grate the rest. Heat some oil for deep-frying to 400°F/200°C and fry the sliced beetroot for about 30 seconds or until crisp. Drain the beetroot crisps on paper towels and lightly salt.

Heat both quantities of stock in a pan and keep warm over a low heat.

Put the olive oil, half the butter and onions for both risottos in a heavy-based pan over a low heat and sauté until soft and translucent, for about 8-10 minutes.

Add both quantities of rice, increase the heat to moderate and stir well to ensure the rice is evenly coated with oil and butter. Remove from the heat.

Transfer about a third of the rice mixture to another pan over a moderate heat, add the red wine and let it evaporate before adding any stock. Stir in the beetroot.

Put the second pan, containing the remaining two-thirds of the rice mixture, back onto a moderate heat, add the white wine and let it evaporate. Stir in the lemon juice and half the lemon zest, reserving the rest to use as a garnish.

Bring the pan of stock to a low boil and keep it simmering whilst making the risottos. Start adding the hot stock to both pans, a ladleful at a time, stirring continuously, for about 15-20 minutes. The beetroot risotto will need about half the amount that the lemon risotto uses. Make sure that each ladle of stock is completely absorbed before adding any more and that the rice is always just covered with liquid. When cooked, the rice should be tender on the outside but with a firm bite on the inside. The risotto should have a soft and runny consistency.

Season well. Beat the remaining butter into both risottos and add the mascarpone to the lemon risotto.

Put a spoonful of each risotto on a plate, garnish each with a beetroot crisp and some of the reserved lemon zest. Serve immediately with grated parmesan.

Advance preparation: fry the beetroot crisps, store in an airtight container; grate the beetroot, sauté the onions, cover and chill up to 1 day before. Heat the onion before adding the rice. Zest and juice the lemons up to 4 hours before, cover and chill. Make the risottos to order.
Freezing: not suitable.

Lemon & beetroot risottos

Jambalaya

This peppery Cajun dish, derived from the Spanish paella, is amongst my favourite one-pot dishes. As I always have rice, onions, garlic and some sort of salami in my storecupboard, it's a good dish for impromptu entertaining. Any missing vegetables are substituted with whatever I happen to have in the fridge. SERVES 10

10oz/275g [1½ cups] red Camargue rice
10oz/275g [1½ cups] long-grain rice
1 large onion, roughly chopped
3 medium cloves garlic, crushed
6floz/175ml olive oil
3 yellow or red sweet peppers, seeded &
    cut into chunky pieces
12oz/350g Spanish chorizo, or other
    spicy sausage, cut into ½in/1cm slices
12oz/350g button mushrooms
11oz/315g large peeled raw prawns or
    shrimps
1¼ pints/725ml [3 cups] chicken stock
2 tblsp chopped thyme
Salt & freshly ground black pepper

Boil the red Camargue rice in a pan of boiling salted water for about 30 minutes and the long-grain rice in a separate pan for 10-12 minutes. When cooked, both should still have a little bite to them. Drain in a colander.

Fry the onion and garlic in 2 tablespoons of the oil in a large pan over a medium heat for 4-5 minutes. Add the peppers, cook for 3 minutes and then transfer the pan's contents to a bowl.

Sauté the chorizo over a high heat for 1 minute, stirring all the time, and add to the onion mixture.

Pour half of the remaining oil into the pan and sauté the mushrooms over a high heat for 2-3 minutes. Remove with a slotted spoon and add to the bowl.

Sauté the prawns very quickly in the remaining oil, still over a high heat, for 1-3 minutes until just cooked. Remove and add to the other ingredients.

Put the stock in the pan, bring to the boil, then stir in the rice and the rest of the

left Jambalaya

ingredients, including the thyme. Heat the jambalaya for 5-6 minutes until hot. Season well before serving.

Advance preparation: sauté the onions, garlic, peppers, mushrooms and chop the thyme up to 1 day before, cover and chill. Make the jambalaya to order.
Freezing: not suitable.

Scallop & coriander kedgeree

Traditionally, kedgeree, also known as khichri, was an Indian mixture of leftover rice or lentils with onions and spices. British colonials then added haddock and it became a classic English breakfast dish. My version has those tiny slate-coloured French lentils, seared scallops and a handful of coriander. Make it for brunch, lunch or supper and serve with a green salad. SERVES 10

10oz/275g [1½ cups] Puy lentils
1lb/450g [2½ cups] basmati rice
30 small scallops
4 tblsp olive oil
1 large onion, sliced
2oz/50g [4 tblsp] butter
1 rounded tsp cumin
1 rounded tsp garam masala
1 pint/570ml [2½ cups] fish or chicken
  stock
2 tblsp chopped coriander [cilantro]
4 hard-boiled eggs, roughly chopped
10 lemon wedges
Mango chutney
Salt & freshly ground black pepper

Put the lentils in a bowl, cover with boiling water and leave for 2 hours to soak. Drain, transfer to a pan of fresh water and boil for about 15-20 minutes until tender. Drain again.
Wash the rice in several changes of cold water and drain well.
Sauté the scallops in batches in hot oil over a high heat for about 1-2 minutes until just cooked.
Fry the onion in butter in a large pan over a low heat for 5-6 minutes, stirring often. Raise the heat to medium and cook for 10-12 minutes or until brown and crispy.

Scallop & coriander kedgeree

Stir in the cumin and garam masala and cook for 1 minute. Add the rice and stock, bring to the boil, stir and cover.
Reduce the heat to low and cook for 10 minutes, by which time most of the liquid will have been absorbed.
Mix in the lentils, coriander, scallops and heat through for 3-4 minutes until hot. Season well and serve, garnished with

chopped egg and lemon wedges. Serve with mango chutney.

Advance preparation: cook the lentils, fry the onions, hard-boil the eggs and chop the coriander up to 1 day before, cover and chill. Make the kedgeree to order.
Freezing: not suitable.

Penne with tomatoes & basil gremolata

This simple pasta salad is for serious garlic lovers. Using really good olive oil makes a big difference to the end result. Here I serve it cold, but there's no reason why it can't be served hot. SERVES 10

10 plum or salad tomatoes
10 tblsp basil leaves, torn
Grated zest of 5 lemons
5 medium cloves garlic, finely chopped
1 tsp Maldon or flaked sea salt
1½lb/700g penne or similar pasta shape
6floz/175ml extra virgin olive oil
3 rounded tblsp capers in balsamic
   vinegar
Freshly ground black pepper

Put the tomatoes into a bowl, pour over boiling water to cover and leave for 10 seconds. Plunge them into cold water, peel off the skins, quarter then remove and discard the seeds. Roughly chop the tomato flesh.

Mix the basil, lemon zest, garlic and flaked salt together for the gremolata.

Cook the pasta in a large pan of salted boiling water for 7-10 minutes until al dente. Drain, rinse quickly under running cold water to stop the cooking, drain again really well and transfer to a bowl to cool.

Pour over the olive oil, mix in the tomatoes and capers and season. Scatter over the gremolata and serve.

Advance preparation: chop the tomatoes, cook the pasta, zest the lemons and chop the garlic up to 4 hours before, cover and chill. Assemble up to 1 hour before serving.
Freezing: not suitable.

Asian ravioli with soy-butter sauce

Instead of making my own ravioli dough, I use won-ton skins. SERVES 10

5 sprigs parsley or coriander [cilantro]
Vegetable oil, for deep-frying
60 won-ton wrappers
1 tblsp cornflour [cornstarch]
2 x Shiitake Mushroom & Ginger Filling
   Recipe (page 40)
for the soy-butter sauce
7floz/200ml red wine vinegar
3½floz/100ml beef stock
3½floz/100ml light soy sauce
14oz/400g [1½ cups] unsalted butter
4 tblsp lemon juice
Salt & freshly ground black pepper

Heat some oil for deep-frying to 400°F/200°C. Deep-fry the parsley or coriander for about 30 seconds until crisp, then drain well on paper towels.

Lay the won-ton wrappers out on a surface lightly dusted with cornflour. Brush the edges with water.

Divide the mushroom mixture between half the wrappers, placing it in the centre. Cover these with a second won-ton wrapper and press the edges together.

Make the sauce by vigorously boiling the vinegar, stock and soy sauce together in a pan until reduced by half.

Dice the butter and whisk it into the sauce over a moderate heat, a piece at a time, to make a creamy emulsion. Add the lemon juice and season to taste.

Penne with tomatoes & basil gremolata

Remove from the heat and keep the sauce hot by sitting it over a pan of warm water.

Poach the ravioli in batches in a large pan of boiling salted water for 2 minutes until light and plump. Remove with a slotted spoon.

Arrange the ravioli on a dish, drizzle over the soy-butter sauce and garnish with the deep-fried parsley or coriander. Serve.

Advance preparation: fill the ravioli up to 4 hours before and put onto a tray dusted with cornflour, cover and chill. Fry the parsley; make the sauce up to 1 hour before and keep warm. Poach the ravioli to order.

Freezing: make and freeze the mushroom mixture up to 4 weeks ahead.

Bacon & egg linguine

A fantastic combination: the best of British coupled with the best of Italy. SERVES 10

11oz/315g pancetta or thinly cut streaky bacon
1lb10oz/750g dried linguine or spaghetti
10 large eggs
Olive oil, for frying
5floz/150ml extra virgin olive oil
9oz/250g [2½ cups] parmesan, grated
2 tblsp chopped parsley
Salt & freshly ground black pepper

Dry-fry the pancetta in a hot pan for 2-3 minutes or until very crisp. Drain on paper towels and crumble. Keep warm in an oven set to 325°F/170°C/Gas 3.

Cook the pasta in a large pan of boiling water for 7-10 minutes or until al dente.

Fry the eggs for 2-3 minutes in hot oil over a medium heat, keeping the yolk runny. Keep warm at the side of the stove.

Drain the pasta, transfer to a dish and pour over the extra virgin olive oil. Add the parmesan, lots of seasoning and toss.

Divide between individual bowls, put a fried egg on top of each then some pancetta and parsley. Serve immediately.

Advance preparation: cook the bacon; chop the parsley 1 day before, cover and chill. Cook the pasta and eggs to order.
Freezing: cook and freeze the pancetta 4 weeks ahead. Crisp up in a hot oven at 375°F/190°C/Gas 5 for 3-4 minutes.

Laksa noodle salad

Laksa is a glorious Singaporean broth, made from a spice paste and enriched with coconut milk before adding rice noodles, beansprouts and vegetables. Here, I use the laksa as a dressing and top the noodles with crisp, raw vegetables. SERVES 10

2 tblsp vegetable oil
5floz/150ml coconut milk
2 large carrots
1lb/450g wide rice noodles
1 cucumber
4oz/100g [1 cup] beansprouts
A few tat-soi leaves, to garnish
for the laksa paste
1 small onion, chopped
1 large clove garlic, crushed
2 tsp finely grated ginger
1 stalk lemon grass, white part only
½oz/15g [2 tblsp] macadamia nuts or
   candlenuts
½ tsp shrimp paste or blachan
1 tsp hot red chilli flakes
½ tsp turmeric
½ tsp ground coriander
½ tsp ground cumin

Grind all the laksa paste ingredients together, either with a pestle and mortar, or in a food processor until smooth.
Fry the paste in oil over a medium heat for 2-3 minutes. Lower the heat, pour in the coconut milk and cook for 5 minutes until the mixture is the consistency of thick pouring cream. Cool.
Cut the carrots and cucumber into paper-thin shavings with a vegetable peeler. Put the carrot shavings into a bowl of iced water and leave for 30 minutes so that they curl. Drain well on paper towels.
Put the noodles in a bowl, pour over boiling water, soak for 5 minutes and then drain and pat dry carefully. Transfer to a serving dish.
Toss the noodles in the laksa paste, or alternatively, spoon it over the noodles. Strew the vegetables, beansprouts and tat-soi over the top and serve.

Advance preparation: make and fry the laksa paste with the coconut milk up to 4 days before, cover and chill. Prepare the carrots and put into water; cut the cucumber up to 6 hours ahead, cover and chill. Assemble the salad up to 1 hour before, cover and chill.
Freezing: not suitable.

Crispy noodle chicken salad

This Asian-style salad has lovely clean, fresh-tasting flavours, perfect for hot summer days. SERVES 10

for the salad
Vegetable oil, for deep-frying
5oz/150g rice sticks
1 tblsp toasted sesame oil
9oz/250g fresh shiitake mushrooms
1lb/450g baby corn
1lb2oz/500g cooked chicken breast,
   thinly sliced
14oz/400g cooked prawns or shrimps,
   shelled & deveined
9oz/250g [2¼ cups] beansprouts
5 spring onions [scallions], sliced
   diagonally
Salt
for the dressing
6 tblsp lime juice
4 tblsp Thai fish sauce
4 tblsp red wine vinegar
2 medium-sized hot red chillies, seeded
   & thinly sliced
1 medium clove garlic, crushed
1 rounded tsp sugar

Heat some oil for deep-frying to 375°F/190°C. Deep-fry the rice sticks in batches for 30 seconds until puffed up and lightly coloured.
Lift out onto paper towels to drain, sprinkle liberally with salt whilst still hot, then leave to cool.
Heat a wok or sauté pan, pour in the sesame oil and fry the mushrooms for 2 minutes over a medium heat until cooked but firm. Drain on paper towels.
Cook the corn in boiling water for 3 minutes or until just tender. Drain and refresh in cold water then drain well on paper towels.
Mix all the ingredients together for the salad dressing.

Laksa noodle salad

Put the rice sticks in a serving dish, toss the rest of the salad ingredients in the dressing and arrange them in a separate dish. Serve.

Advance preparation: cook the rice sticks, mushrooms, corn, chicken and prawns and make the dressing up to 1 day in advance. Store the noodles in an airtight container and everything else separately covered in the fridge. Assemble up to 2 hours before.
Freezing: not suitable.

Buckwheat noodles with chestnuts & wild mushrooms

Vacuum-packed chestnuts are a godsend as they are so time-consuming to prepare otherwise. Their earthy, sweet nutty taste complements the wild mushrooms and noodles splendidly. SERVES 10

1lb/450g mixed wild mushrooms
5oz/150g [10 tblsp] butter
14oz/400g vacuum-packed chestnuts
2 large cloves garlic, crushed

1½ pints/850ml double cream [3½ cups heavy cream]
5 tblsp chopped parsley
2 tblsp lemon juice
12oz/350g buckwheat noodles
Salt & freshly ground black pepper

Sauté the mushrooms in batches in the butter over a high heat for 3-4 minutes. Set aside. Sauté the chestnuts and garlic for 2 minutes in the same pan.
Return the mushrooms to the pan with the chestnuts and add the cream. Bring to

the boil, lower the heat and simmer for 2 minutes. Stir in the parsley, lemon juice and seasoning .
Boil the noodles in a large pan of water for 4 minutes or until al dente. Drain, pour over the mushroom sauce, stir and serve.

Advance preparation: make the mushroom sauce up to 4 hours ahead, cover and chill. Reheat over a low heat for 5-7 minutes, adding a little water if necessary. Cook the noodles to order. *Freezing: not suitable.*

the menu

Vodka cherry tomatoes with herbed garlic salt

Sesame cheese straws

Parmesan toasts

Anchovy pastries

Curry puffs

Crispy noodle chicken salad

Oriental coleslaw

Cucumber, sugar snap & radish salad

Mojito

Watermelon frappé

Clockwise from top right:
fruity frappés offer refreshment on hot days; Oriental Coleslaw is an exotic twist on a traditional picnic favourite; pack food in disposable cartons for easy eating, and because you will not want to wash up after a fun day out; fresh chillies add bite to Crispy Noodle Chicken Salad; when everything is easy to carry and clear up you will resolve to have picnics more often.

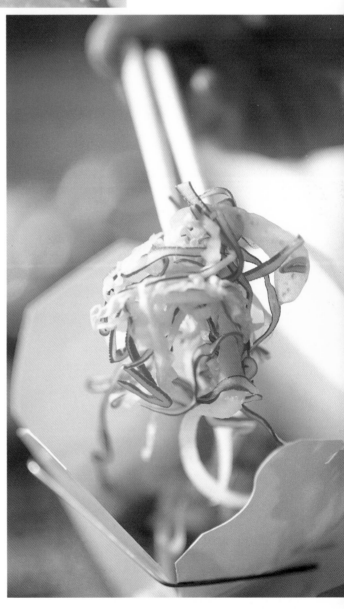

picnic

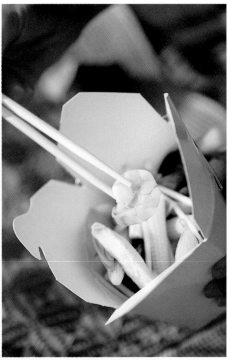

Clockwise from top right:
*chopsticks make convenient picnic
utensils; so do fingers (here used
to dip marinated cherry tomatoes
in herby salt); Curry Puffs are
quickly made from bought pastry
and your favourite curry paste;
take a box of tasty crispy things
to snack on throughout the day;
a fresh salad of cucumber, sugar
snaps and radishes complements
the noodle dish; Mojito, a good
hot weather drink, served in cups.*

Green salad

The contents of a green salad are very much a matter of personal preference and depend on what you plan to serve it with. You ideally want a mixture of something peppery like rocket [arugula], mustard greens or watercress; something mild, which might be lamb's lettuce or baby spinach; and something bitter such as chicory [Belgian endive], or curly endive. Then, I like to throw in a delicate leaf such as pourpier, which looks like a tiny lily pad with a speck of a white flower. Herbs – chervil, basil, coriander [cilantro], and so on – can also be added, however do not overdo the choice of leaves or you will have lots of competing flavours in the salad. Three, or four, maximum, varieties will do. Always tear leaves, never cut them, and wash and dry them really well so as not to dilute the dressing. Dressings, too, can be varied, but if the salad is to accompany another dish, or several dishes, I tend to use fruity olive oil and balsamic or wine vinegar. SERVES 10

5oz/150g mixed salad leaves
2 tblsp balsamic vinegar
4 tblsp extra virgin olive oil
Salt & freshly ground black pepper

Tear all the salad leaves into bite-sized pieces.
Grind salt and pepper into the vinegar, then mix in the oil.
Toss the salad greens in the dressing and serve immediately.

Advance preparation: make the dressing up to 2 days ahead, cover. Wash, dry, but do not tear the salad, up to 1 day before, cover and chill. Toss in the dressing to order.
Freezing: not suitable.

right Green mango & papaya salad

Tomato salad

To make this bold, beautiful salad, choose lots of different varieties of tomato. Stripy green, orange, big ones, little ones, shiny red and sunny yellow. You could even throw in a few home-roasted tomatoes. Then all they need is a perfectly simple olive oil dressing and a few fresh herbs. SERVES 10

2½lb/1.15kg mixed tomatoes, such
   as beefsteak, cherry, heirloom &
   plum varieties
5 tblsp extra virgin olive oil
1 tbslp balsamic vinegar
1 rounded tblsp basil, marjoram
   or oregano leaves
Maldon or flaked sea salt
Freshly ground black pepper

Slice the large tomatoes, halve the medium-sized tomatoes and leave the small tomatoes whole. Arrange them all in a serving dish.
Mix the oil and balsamic vinegar together with some salt and pepper. Drizzle the dressing over the tomatoes and sprinkle with the herbs. Serve.

Advance preparation: make the dressing up to 2 days before; prepare and arrange the tomatoes up to 3 hours ahead, cover and chill. Remove from the fridge 1 hour before serving; dress, add herbs and cover 30 minutes before.
Freezing: not suitable.

Cucumber, sugar snap & radish salad

To ring the changes, substitute toasted sesame seeds for the peanuts. SERVES 10

for the salad
9oz/250g sugar snap peas
2 cucumbers, peeled
5 radishes, cut into thin strips
1oz/25g [3 tblsp] unsalted peanuts,
   toasted & roughly chopped
for the rice wine vinegar dressing
2 tblsp rice wine vinegar or white wine
   vinegar
1 rounded tsp salt
1 rounded tsp sugar

Cook the sugar snap peas in boiling water for 2-3 minutes so that they retain some crispness.

Drain and refresh in cold water until stone cold to preserve the colour. Dry on paper towels and split in half.

Cut the cucumbers lengthways into quarters, cut away the seeds and slice into chunky diagonal pieces.

Place in a serving dish, add the rice vinegar, salt and sugar and mix well. Leave for 10 minutes to let the flavours marry, stirring once or twice.

Add the sugar snaps, radishes and peanuts just before serving so the vinegar does not discolour the sugar snaps.

Advance preparation: toast and chop the peanuts up to 2 days ahead, keep covered; prepare the rest of the salad ingredients up to 8 hours ahead, cover and keep chilled in separate containers. *Freezing: not suitable*

Green mango & papaya salad

It is worth trying to track down palm sugar which can be found in Asian food stores and is sold as a syrup. A staple of South-East Asian cooking, it is made from the boiled sap of coconut and palmyrah palms and has a dark, deep sweetness which enhances salads like this one no end. Use it to acompany the Red Duck Curry (page 99). SERVES 10

1lb5oz/600g green mangoes
1¾lb/800g green papaya
1 small coconut, shelled
5 tblsp coriander [cilantro] leaves
5 tblsp mint leaves
5 tblsp Thai basil leaves
for the dressing
2 tblsp palm sugar, or dark brown sugar
1 tblsp boiling water
6 tblsp lime juice
1 tblsp Thai fish sauce
Salt & freshly ground black pepper

Mix all the dressing ingredients together, stirring until the sugar dissolves.

Finely shred the mango and papaya into thin matchsticks.

Remove a third of the coconut and use a vegetable peeler to cut it into shavings for decoration. Shave the remainder and then shred it into thin matchsticks.

Toss the fruits, coconut matchsticks and herbs together in the dressing. Arrange in a dish, scatter over the reserved coconut shavings and serve.

Advance preparation: make the dressing up to 2 days ahead, cover and chill. Cut the mango, papaya and coconut up to 4 hours before, cover and chill. Assemble the salad up to 30 minutes before, cover and chill. *Freezing: not suitable.*

Oriental coleslaw

This crisp, pretty coleslaw with its light citrus-soy dressing is very quick and simple to make. SERVES 10

for the coleslaw
10½oz/300g red cabbage
14oz/400g Chinese leaves [Napa cabbage]
14oz/400g fennel
for the oriental dressing
6 tblsp orange juice
4 tblsp rice wine vinegar
2 tblsp light soy sauce
4 tsp finely grated ginger

Finely shred the cabbage, Chinese leaves and fennel.

Mix all the ingredients together for the dressing and pour over the coleslaw just 15 minutes before serving to prevent the salad from wilting.

Transfer to a salad bowl and serve.

Advance preparation: make the dressing up to 2 days ahead, cover and chill. Prepare the vegetables up to 3 hours before and keep covered in the fridge. *Freezing: not suitable.*

Rocket, french bean, red onion & croûton salad

Serve this substantial salad on its own, or with a plate of charcuterie, for lunch or supper. SERVES 10

5 small red onions, quartered through
  the root
6floz/175ml olive oil
2 tblsp red wine vinegar
10oz/275g rustic bread, such as
  ciabatta, pugliese or sourdough
5oz/150g French beans [haricot verts]
3oz/75g rocket [arugula] leaves
3oz/75g [½ cup] mixed olives, such as
  niçoise, Kalamata & green
1oz/25g [2½ tblsp] capers
Salt & freshly ground black pepper
for the garlic dressing
1½ tblsp red wine vinegar
1 clove garlic, crushed
4½ tblsp olive oil

Make the dressing by grinding salt and pepper into the vinegar. Add the garlic and then the oil. Mix and leave for 30 minutes to infuse.

Heat the oven to 375°F/190°C/Gas 5. Put the onions on a baking tray and drizzle them with 2 tablespoons of the olive oil and the red wine vinegar. Cook for 25 minutes or until soft and tender.

Cut the bread, including the crust, into chunky 1in/2.5cm cubes. Put them onto a baking tray, moisten with the rest of the olive oil and bake for 10-15 minutes until golden, shaking them occasionally. Drain on paper towels and season with salt.

Cook the beans in boiling salted water for 3-4 minutes, or until tender but still with some bite. Drain, then refresh in cold water until stone cold. Dry the beans on paper towels and cut diagonally in half.

Put all the salad ingredients into a bowl, add the dressing and toss well. Serve.

Advance preparation: make the croûtons up to 4 days before and cover. Warm them in a preheated oven set to

left Rocket, french bean, red onion & croûton salad

350°F/180°C/Gas 4 for 5 minutes to freshen up. Make the dressing up to 2 days ahead; roast the onions; cook the beans; wash and dry the rocket up to 1 day before, cover and chill. Toss the salad to order.

Freezing: make and freeze the croûtons up to 4 weeks ahead. Crisp up, as above.

Potato, watercress & walnut salad

The Chicken Tonnato (page 96) and Roast Beef Salad (page 95) would be splendid main courses to serve with this peppery watercress and potato salad. SERVES 10

1lb2oz/500g small waxy potatoes
12oz/350g watercress
4oz/110g [1 cup] walnuts
Salt & freshly ground black pepper
for the walnut oil dressing
3 tblsp red wine or cider vinegar
2 tsp Dijon mustard
4 tblsp walnut oil

Make the dressing by mixing the vinegar and mustard together in a small bowl with some salt. Stir in the oil.
Cook the potatoes in boiling salted water for 10-12 minutes, or until tender. Drain, cool a little, cut in half and then pour over half the dressing and mix well. The potatoes will absorb more flavour if you do this whilst they are still hot. Season.
Toss the potatoes, warm or cold, watercress and walnuts together in the remaining dressing and serve.

Advance preparation: make the dressing up to 2 days before; cook and dress the potatoes (if serving cold) up to 1 day ahead, cover and chill. Toss the salad to order.
Freezing: not suitable.

Mozzarella with olives, anchovies & parsley

Mozzarella with olives, anchovies & parsley

I always think mozzarella needs a helping hand and should be teamed with distinctively flavoured ingredients. The Olive & Parsley salad is ideal for this purpose. This dish is a good accompaniment to some sliced prosciutto di Parma and can be served as a first course or lunch dish. SERVES 10

2 x Olive & Parsley Salad, made without lemon zest (page 42)
1½oz/40g [⅓ cup] sun-dried tomatoes in oil, roughly chopped
1oz/25g anchovies, roughly chopped
4 balls mozzarella, each sliced into 5
2 tblsp olive oil

Make the olive & parsley salad the same way as on page 42, but chop everything much less finely. Add the sun-dried tomatoes and anchovies and mix well.
Arrange the mozzarella on a platter, spoon over the olive-parsley mixture and drizzle with the oil. Serve.

Advance preparation: refer to the Olive-Parsley Salad recipe. Chop the sun-dried tomatoes and anchovies and store separately, covered, in the fridge up to 1 day before. Combine the olive-parsley salad up to 4 hours ahead and assemble with the cheese up to 30 minutes before, cover and chill.
Freezing: not suitable.

Roasted vegetables

Everyone adores roasted vegetables and this dish is no exception. The vegetables are sweet, sticky and crisp all at the same time. Try them with the Chicken Scaloppine (page 97), omitting the roasted red and yellow cherry tomatoes in that recipe, or serve them as a simple main course supper dish in their own right with good bread. SERVES 10

5 plum tomatoes, halved lengthways
6floz/180ml olive oil
A large pinch of sugar
1½lb/700g sweet potato, cut into chunks
1½lb/700g parsnips, cut into chunks
1lb/450g shallots, halved lengthways
 if large
12oz/350g small field or meadow
 mushrooms
2 tsp thyme leaves
Salt & freshly ground black pepper

Heat the oven to 190°C/375°F/Gas 5. Put the tomatoes skin-side down in a roasting pan, drizzle with 2 tablespoons of the olive oil and sprinkle with the sugar, plus some salt and pepper.

Roast the tomatoes for 30 minutes or until soft and slightly charred. Remove them from the pan whilst warm, lift onto paper towels and set aside.

Raise the temperature of the oven to 400°F/200°C/Gas 6. Divide the sweet potato, parsnips and shallots between 2 roasting pans and toss the vegetables in 4floz/120ml of the olive oil.

Roast them for 45-60 minutes, turning and basting the vegetables halfway through cooking and swapping the pans between the shelves at the same time.

Toss the mushrooms and thyme in the remaining oil. Add them and the roasted tomatoes to the other vegetables and roast for a further 15 minutes, until everything is tender and golden.

Drain all the vegetables on paper towels, then season to taste and serve.

Advance preparation: roast, cool and chill the tomatoes 2 days before. Cook the sweet potato, parsnips and shallots 4 hours before. Reheat them to order at 400°F/200°C/Gas 6 for 20 minutes, adding the mushrooms, thyme and roast tomatoes to the pans 5 minutes later. *Freezing: not suitable.*

Stir-fried bok choy, asparagus & sugar snaps

You could add, or substitute, shiitake mushrooms, baby corn, Chinese leaves [Napa cabbage] or beansprouts to those vegetables I've already suggested here. The Red Duck Curry (page 99) and Asian Ravioli (page 118) would benefit from being served with this quick dish. SERVES 10

1lb/450g small bok choy, halved
 lengthways
1lb/450g asparagus, halved diagonally
9oz/250g spring onions [scallions], split
 lengthways
9oz/250g sugar snap peas
2in/5cm piece ginger, cut into fine strips
2 cloves garlic, crushed
2 tblsp toasted sesame oil
2 tblsp Thai fish sauce
1 tsp palm sugar, or dark brown sugar

Toss all the vegetables together with the ginger and garlic.

Heat the oil in a wok or large pan over a high heat. Add the vegetables and stir-fry for about 2-3 minutes, constantly moving the vegetables around the pan.

Add the fish sauce and palm sugar, stir some more and cook for another 30 seconds, so the vegetables are still crisp. Serve immediately.

Advance preparation: prepare all the vegetables, ginger and garlic up to 8 hours ahead and keep separate, covered in the fridge. Stir-fry to order. *Freezing: not suitable.*

Roasted vegetables

Borlotti & green beans

If you omit the butter, you can serve these beans cold as a salad, tossed in a trickle of extra virgin olive oil and balsamic vinegar. Scour the shops for different types of beans and use whatever is best that day. Snake, yellow and fresh butter or lima beans will be fine too. SERVES 10

1½lb/700g fresh borlotti beans, shelled to yield 4oz/110g
12oz/350g runner beans [pole beans]
12oz/350g bobby beans [round green beans]
12oz/350g French beans [haricot verts]
1¼lb/570g broad beans [fava beans], shelled to yield 4oz/110g
2oz/50g butter [4 tblsp], melted
Salt & freshly ground black pepper

Put the borlotti beans in a pan of cold unsalted water and bring to the boil. Lower the heat, cover and simmer for 45-60 minutes or until tender.

Remove the beans with a slotted spoon, drain and dry on paper towels.

Use the same large pan of boiling salted water to cook the rest of the beans until they are tender but still have some bite. Top up with more boiling water during cooking if necessary. Cook the beans in the following order and for the following amount of time: runner and bobby beans 4-6 minutes; french beans 3-4 minutes; broad beans 2-3 minutes.

Drain all the beans in a colander under cold running water to preserve the colour. Dry on paper towels.

Heat the oven to 375°F/190°C/Gas 5. Peel the broad beans, discarding the skins.

Toss all the cooked beans in the melted butter, season and put into an ovenproof serving dish. Cover and heat in the oven for 12-15 minutes or until hot. Serve.

Advance preparation: cook all the beans up to 1 day ahead, cover and chill. Toss in the butter and season up to 4 hours before and cover. Heat as above.
Freezing: not suitable.

right Stir-fried bok choy, asparagus & sugar snaps

Red berry kissel with biscotti & vanilla cream

I have made this kissel for years now and never tire of it. It is a luscious compôte of soft red fruits and I use it in lots of different ways. Try it on hot waffles with a scoop of ice-cream, spooned onto sweet bruschetta bread or on hot cinnamon toast with lashings of clotted cream. I've also had great success when I've used it as a filling for summer puddings and as a topping for a tart filled with sweetened mascarpone. When brides want to serve their chocolate sachertorte wedding cake (page 141) as a dessert, this kissel accompanies it exquisitely. In winter, any frozen berries (apart from strawberries) work successfully. Serve the kissel with something crisp like Italian biscotti or a deep-fried won-ton wrapper dusted with cinnamon and sugar (page 78). SERVES 10

20 biscotti

for the kissel

12oz/350g [3 cups] raspberries

4 tblsp water

4oz/110g [heaped ½ cup] sugar + extra
  to taste

5floz/150ml fresh orange juice

1 pint/570ml [2½ cups] red wine

1 rounded tblsp cornflour [cornstarch]

3lb/1.35kg mixed soft berries, such as
  blackberries, pitted cherries, red, black
  & white currants, raspberries &
  strawberries

for the vanilla cream

1 vanilla bean, split lengthways

10floz/275ml double cream [heavy
  cream]

1 tblsp caster sugar [granulated sugar]

Put the raspberries, water and sugar for the kissel in a pan and cook over a low heat for 3-4 minutes, until the raspberries just begin to soften. Remove from the heat, purée in a food processor and then sieve to remove the seeds.

Put the raspberry purée, orange juice and wine in a pan and bring to the boil.

Take 3 tablespoons of the hot liquid and mix it with the cornflour. Add this mixture to the pan, bring to the boil and stir well for 2 minutes or until thickened. Cool the sauce until it is barely warm.

Remove the seeds from the vanilla bean with a teaspoon and add them to the cream with the sugar.

Whisk the cream until soft peaks form, then spoon it into a bowl.

Fold all the prepared fruits, except any strawberries, into the warm sauce and add sugar to taste. Leave to cool and add the strawberries when the sauce is cold. The sauce should lightly coat the fruits. Serve with the cream and biscotti.

Advance preparation: make the kissel, without adding the strawberries, up to 2 days before, cover and chill. Add the strawberries to the kissel and whisk the cream up to 4 hours before, cover and chill. Stir both lightly before serving. *Freezing: freeze the kissel, without the strawberries, up to 4 weeks ahead.*

Baked peaches with figs, ginger & spices

An autumnal dish of baked peaches (you could also use apples), stuffed with dried fruits and nuts and spiced up with stem ginger, nutmeg and cardamom. Serve with some Greek strained yogurt. SERVES 10

1½oz/40g [⅓ cup] hazelnuts

1½oz/40g [3 tblsp] unsalted butter

9oz/250g dried figs, sliced

1½oz/40g [⅓ cup] stem ginger in syrup,
  sliced

½ tsp grated nutmeg

½ tsp ground cardamom

Grated zest & juice of 2 oranges

3½floz/100ml muscat or sweet white wine

10 peaches

Heat the oven to 375°F/190°C/Gas 5. Roast the hazelnuts for 5 minutes and then halve them. Leave the oven on.

Mix together the nuts, butter, figs, ginger, spices, orange zest, juice and wine.

Cut a 1½in/4cm circle around the top of the peaches and then push the knife down to cut around the stone. Twist the stone out, being careful not to damage the flesh of the fruit.

Put the peaches, side by side, in an ovenproof serving dish. Fill the centre of

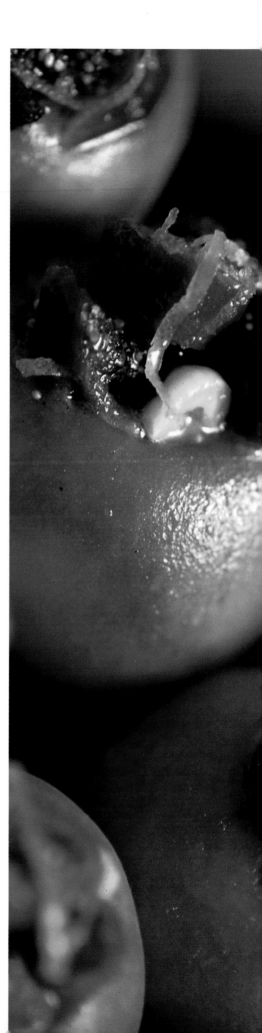

the fruit with the stuffing and pour over any remaining juices. Bake the peaches for 20-25 minutes until soft, then serve.

Advance preparation: make the stuffing up to 3 days ahead, cover and chill. Stuff the peaches up to 4 hours before and bake to order.
Freezing: make and freeze the stuffing up to 4 weeks before.

Rolled pavlova with mango & passionfruit

This is the most divine, melt-in-the-mouth dessert: pure white, soft meringue filled with cream and tropical fruits. Try it in summer months marbled with cream, lemon curd and lots of ripe red berries. SERVES 10

for the pavlova
6 large egg whites
5oz/150g caster sugar [¾ cup superfine sugar]
2oz/50g icing sugar [½ cup confectioners' sugar] + 1 tblsp extra for dusting
1 tblsp cornflour [cornstarch]
for the mango & passionfruit sauce
1 large mango (to yield 10floz/275ml purée)
4 passionfruit, seeds & juice removed
2 tblsp lime juice
1-2 tblsp sugar
for the filling
2 passionfruit, seeds & juice removed
10floz/275ml double cream [heavy cream]
1 large mango, thinly sliced
for the decoration
5floz/150ml double cream [heavy cream], lightly whipped
You will also need a baking tray approximately 15 x 10in (37.5 x 25.5cm), some parchment paper, a piping bag and a ½in/1cm star nozzle

Heat the oven to 375°F/190°C/Gas 5 and line the baking tray with parchment paper.
Whisk the egg whites until they are stiff but not dry.
Sieve together the sugars and cornflour for the pavlova. Whisk them into the egg whites, 1 tablespoon at a time, until the meringue is thick.

Spread the meringue onto the baking tray and smooth the top with a palette knife [metal spatula]. Bake for 8 minutes until light golden, firm and slightly rubbery to touch. Remove the meringue to a wire rack to cool.
Turn the meringue onto a piece of parchment lightly dusted with icing sugar and then peel off the paper on which the meringue was baked.
Blend the mango for the sauce in a food processor until smooth and then sieve. To make the sauce, mix together the mango purée, passionfruit seeds and juice, lime juice and add sugar to taste. Set aside until ready to serve.
Whip lightly the double cream for the filling then fold in the passionfruit seeds and juice. Spread this mixture onto the cooled meringue.
Arrange the sliced mango on top of the cream, reserving 10 slices to decorate.
Roll up the filled pavlova carefully, pushing it away from you and using the parchment to help you do so.
Dust the pavlova with icing sugar and carefully lift it onto a serving dish.
Whip lightly the double cream for the decoration. Pipe rosettes of the cream onto the pavlova and decorate with the reserved slices of mango. Serve with the passionfruit sauce.

Advance preparation: bake the meringue and make the sauce up to 1 day before; chill the meringue, uncovered, and chill the sauce covered. Assemble the pavlova up to 4 hours before, undecorated, cover and chill. Decorate 1 hour before serving.
Freezing: the sauce can be made and frozen up to 4 weeks ahead.

left Baked peaches with figs, ginger & spices

Increase the heat a little, without letting the mixture boil, and whisk until frothy. Keep the chocolate warm.

Add the orange oil and zest to the choux pastry, mix well and transfer the dough to a piping bag with nozzle.

Heat the oil to 350°F/180°C. Pipe the choux pastry into the oil in 4in/10cm loops, only 3 at a time. Turn them once and cook for about 1-1½ minutes, or until crisp and golden.

Drain the churros on paper towels and dredge well with icing sugar.

Pour the hot chocolate into glasses and serve immediately with the churros to dip.

Advance preparation: make the flavoured choux pastry, cover and chill; make, cool, cover and chill the hot chocolate up 1 day before. Heat the hot chocolate over a low heat for 10 minutes and fry the churros to order.

Freezing: make and freeze the flavoured choux pastry up to 4 weeks ahead.

Apple & blackberry filo pastries

Filo pastry is such an asset for making desserts in a hurry. Here, it is topped with wafer-thin slices of apple and strewn with a few ripe blackberries. Keep the filo covered with a clean damp cloth while making this dish to stop it from drying out. SERVES 10

16 sheets filo pastry, measuring about 17½ x 7in/44 x18cm

4oz/110g [½ cup] unsalted butter, melted, + extra for greasing

5 dessert apples, such as Granny Smith, peeled & very finely sliced

10oz/275g [2 cups] blackberries

3 tblsp caster sugar [granulated sugar]

1 tblsp icing sugar [confectioners' sugar]

10floz/275ml double cream [heavy cream], lightly whipped

Brush 1 sheet of pastry with some of the melted butter. Put another sheet on top and brush this lightly with butter too. Continue until you have a total of 8 layers.

Repeat with the remaining pastry and butter to make another stack. Cut each

Orange churros with hot chocolate

Orange churros with hot chocolate

Now, neither the churros, nor the hot chocolate, actually need each other, as both are wonderful in their own right. But the combination of the two is a knockout and just right for serving at brunches when everyone needs something hot and sweet to give their Sunday a kick-start (they are also good for tea or to end a meal). Churros, Spanish breakfast fritters, are often dipped into a cup of coffee. In Spain they make them with a flour and water batter, but mine are made from choux pastry flavoured with orange oil. Specialist food shops sell this orange oil in small bottles. If you can't find it, add extra orange zest to compensate. SERVES 10

for the hot chocolate

1lb2oz/500g dark, semi-sweet chocolate

2½ pints/1.5 litres [1½ quarts] milk

for the orange churros

2 x Choux Pastry recipe (page 81)

1 tsp orange oil

1 tsp grated orange zest

Vegetable oil, for deep-frying

2 tblsp icing sugar [confectioners' sugar]

You will also need a piping bag and ½in/1cm star nozzle.

Break the chocolate into squares and place them in a pan with the milk. Heat them gently over a low setting for about 10 minutes or until the chocolate has completely melted.

stack into 5 rectangles measuring about 3½ x 7in/9 x 18cm.

Arrange the apple in overlapping layers on top of the pastries and divide the blackberries between them. Brush the pastries all over with the remaining butter and sprinkle them with caster sugar.

Heat the oven to 350°F/180°C/Gas 4. Lift the pastries onto 2 lightly greased baking sheets and bake them for 20 minutes or until golden, swapping the trays over in the oven halfway through cooking.

Dust the pastries with icing sugar and serve them with the whipped cream.

Advance preparation: bake the pastries up to 4 hours before and cover. Reheat in a preheated oven at 350°F/180°C/Gas 4 for 5-7 minutes.
Freezing: not suitable.

Apricot tart

This is a lovely, classic French tart. Other stone fruits such as plums and greengages are good used instead of apricots. SERVES 10

⅓ (11oz/300g) x Sweet Shortcrust Pastry Recipe (page 80)
Flour, for dusting
for the filling
3 tblsp ground almonds
20 apricots, halved & stoned
5floz/150ml double cream [heavy cream]
2 large eggs, lightly beaten
5 tblsp vanilla sugar
1½ tsp vanilla extract
2 tblsp icing sugar [confectioners' sugar]
You will also need a 9½in/24cm square or 10in/25.5cm round, shallow, loose-bottomed fluted tart tin, some baking parchment and baking beans

Roll the chilled pastry thinly on a lightly floured surface until it is 2in/5cm larger than the tin.

Wrap the pastry around the rolling pin and let it unroll over the tin, pressing it down into the bottom and up the sides. Roll the pin over the top of the tin to trim away any excess pastry.

Prick the base of the pastry case with a fork and chill for 30 minutes.

Heat the oven to 375°F/190°C/Gas 5. Line the tart with baking parchment and baking beans and bake for 15 minutes until golden. Remove the parchment and beans and bake for a further 5 minutes.

Remove the tart case from the oven and set aside to cool slightly. Lower the oven temperature to 350°F/180°C/Gas 4.

Sprinkle the almonds on the bottom of the tart case and arrange the apricots on top, standing them cut-side up.

Whisk together the cream, eggs, vanilla sugar and extract. Pour this mixture into the tart case and bake for 45-50 minutes, or until the custard has set and the apricots are slightly caramelized.

Cool for 10 minutes before removing the tart from the tin to a serving dish. Dust with icing sugar and serve hot or cold.

Advance preparation: bake the tart case and mix the custard up to 1 day before; store the tart in an airtight box; cover and chill the custard. Bake to order if serving hot, allowing an extra 5 minutes cooking time. If serving cold, bake up to 12 hours ahead, cover and chill. Remove from the fridge 1 hour before serving.
Freezing: the tart case can be frozen unbaked in its tin for up to 1 week and baked straight from the freezer. Freeze it baked up to 3 weeks ahead.

Apple & blackberry filo pastries

Raspberry & lemon syllabub trifle

Trifle, but not as we know it: day-glo jelly, with more bounce than the school trampoline, lumpy custard, jam swiss roll, canned fruits and, of course, the inevitable decoration of maraschino cherries and angelica diamonds. My trifle is a far cry from that and is a sensuous stack of buttery brioche, billowing lemon syllabub, vanilla cream and fresh raspberries. SERVES 10

5 small brioche, each sliced into 4
4 tblsp sweet white wine or sherry
5oz/150g [1¼ cups] raspberries
2 x Lemon Syllabub Recipe (page 81)
1 tblsp icing sugar [confectioners' sugar]
1oz/25g candied cedro, or citrus peel,
  cut into thin shavings

for the raspberry sauce
3oz/75g [⅔ cup] raspberries
1 tblsp water
2 tblsp caster sugar [granulated sugar]

for the vanilla cream
1 vanilla bean, split lengthways
5floz/150ml double cream [heavy cream]
2 tsp caster sugar [granulated sugar]

Make the sauce by heating the raspberries, water and sugar in a pan over a low heat for 3-4 minutes, until the raspberries just begin to soften. **Remove** from the heat and cool. Purée in a food processor and then sieve.

Scrape the seeds from the vanilla bean and add them to the cream with the sugar. Whisk until soft peaks form.

Place a slice of brioche on a dessert plate. Drizzle it with some wine, spoon on some vanilla cream, then a few raspberries and a spoonful of raspberry purée. Top it with another slice of brioche, some more wine and then some syllabub.

Decorate by arranging a few pieces of citrus peel on top and lightly dusting the whole thing with icing sugar. Repeat with the remaining ingredients and serve.

Advance preparation: make the fruit sauce and syllabub up to 1 day before, cover and chill. Whisk the syllabub a little if it separates. Assemble up to 1½ hours before, cover and chill. Remove from the fridge 30 minutes before eating.
Freezing: make and freeze the raspberry sauce up to 4 weeks in advance.

Saffron cream with sesame-poppy seed wafers

Saffron cream with sesame-poppy seed wafers

This saffron cream is the simplest pudding in the world to make and, apart from allowing time for the saffron to infuse, it truly takes just 5 minutes from start to finish. The wafers take a bit longer. They have a real nutty crunch to them, which a dessert as rich as this needs. SERVES 10

for the sesame-poppy seed wafers
1oz/25g [2 tblsp] unsalted butter + extra for greasing
2oz/50g demerara sugar [¼ cup raw brown sugar]
2 tblsp clear honey
¾oz/20g [2 tblsp] poppy seeds
¾oz/20g [2½ tblsp] sesame seeds
for the saffron cream
3 tblsp warm milk
18-20 saffron threads
1¼ pints/725ml [3 cups] crème fraîche
2½oz/60g [5 tblsp] sugar

Put the butter, sugar and honey in a pan and bring to the boil. Add the sesame and poppy seeds, stir well and remove from the heat to completely cool and firm up.

Heat the oven to 400°F/200°C/Gas 6. Divide the mixture into 20 small balls. Place them well apart on lightly greased baking trays and flatten with your thumb.

Bake for about 5 minutes, or until slightly darker in colour. Remove the wafers to a wire rack to cool and harden.

Mix the milk and saffron threads together and leave to infuse for 10 minutes.

Place the crème fraîche and sugar in a bowl and pour on the saffron milk. Whisk with an electric beater at a high speed for 1½ minutes until light and aerated.

Spoon the saffron cream into a dish and serve with 2 wafers per person.

Advance preparation: make the saffron cream 4 days before, cover and chill. Stir before serving. Make the wafers 3 days before and store in an airtight container.
Freezing: make and freeze the wafers up to 4 weeks ahead, layered between parchment paper. Crisp up, if needed, in a preheated oven at 400°F/200°C/Gas 6 for 2 minutes. Cool before serving.

Chocolate mousse with espresso granita & stencilled cookies

Chocolate, coffee and more chocolate. This is a very decadent pudding of dark chocolate mousse, rich heavy cream and bitter espresso coffee granita. And then, just to gild the lily, there are some frivolous stencilled chocolate cookies to go with it. SERVES 10

10floz/275ml Jersey double cream [rich heavy cream], lightly whipped

for the espresso granita
2oz/50g [¼ cup] sugar
5floz/150ml boiling water
5floz/150ml very strong espresso coffee

for the stencilled cookies
⅓ (9½oz/265g) x Chocolate Cookie Dough Recipe (page 84)
Flour, for dusting
2 tblsp icing sugar [confectioners' sugar]

for the chocolate mousse
12oz/350g dark, semi-sweet chocolate, broken into squares
3½floz/100ml very strong espresso coffee
1 tblsp orange liqueur, such as Cointreau or Grand Marnier
½oz/15g [1 tblsp] unsalted butter
3 large egg yolks, separated
1 large egg white
You will also need a 2¾in/7cm round cutter, some parchment paper, an artist's knife or scalpel and an ice-cream scoop

Make the granita by dissolving the sugar in the boiling water, then stirring in the coffee. Cool and pour into a shallow metal tray. Freeze for 1 hour.

Break up the ice-crystals with a fork, mixing them into any unfrozen coffee. Repeat every hour for 3 hours. Fork through the granita to give loose crystals.

Roll the chocolate cookie dough out to a thickness of ¼in/5mm on a lightly floured surface. Stamp out 20 circles using the cutter and transfer to baking trays. Chill for 30 minutes.

Melt the chocolate for the mousse in a large bowl over a pan of simmering water for about 10 minutes. Cool, add the coffee and liqueur, then beat in the butter and the egg yolks, one at a time.

Whisk the egg whites until stiff but not dry and fold them into the chocolate mousse. Pour the mousse into bowl of approximately 1 pint/570ml [2½ cup] capacity, then cover and chill.

Heat the oven to 350°F/180°C/Gas 4 and bake the cookies for 8 minutes until slightly darker in colour. Lift them onto a wire rack to cool.

Make a stencil out of some parchment paper by cutting a 4in/10cm square and then marking a 2¾in/7cm circle in pen on this square. Draw ½in/1cm circles all over this circle, starting from the middle and leaving space in-between. Carefully cut these small circles out using a small artist's knife or scalpel.

Use the same method to make a striped stencil by drawing lines along the paper and cutting out every second strip.

Put the icing sugar into a fine sieve, lay a stencil over a cookie and lightly dust with the icing sugar. Carefully remove the stencil and repeat with half the remaining cookies. Use the other stencil to decorate the last batch of cookies.

Scoop up some chocolate mousse and place in the bottom of an individual glass serving bowl. Cover the mousse with a dollop of whipped cream and finish with a spoonful of granita.

Repeat with the remaining ingredients and serve immediately with the cookies.

Advance preparation: make the chocolate mousse 3 days before, cover and chill. Bake the cookies 2 days before and store in an airtight box; decorate 4 hours before and store uncovered. *Freezing: freeze the cookies 3 weeks before; crisp up in a preheated oven at 350°F/180°C/Gas 4 for 3-4 minutes. Make the granita 3 days before.*

Chocolate mousse with espresso granita & stencilled cookies

Lime & pistachio kulfi with pistachio wafers

Lime & pistachio kulfi with pistachio wafers

Kulfi, much-loved in India, is unlike other ice-creams in that it needs no churning whatsover: it's just a matter of mixing everything together and putting it in the freezer. I like to serve kulfi with translucent pistachio wafers. For an exotic, authentic touch, decorate each ice-cream with a sheet of edible silver leaf available from specialist art shops. SERVES 10

for the lime & pistachio kulfi

5oz/150g [1 cup] unsalted, peeled
  pistachio nuts

1 tblsp finely grated lime zest

6 tblsp caster sugar [granulated sugar]

8floz/225ml lime juice

1 pint/570ml [2½ cups] canned
  evaporated milk

8floz/225ml milk

A few drops of green food colouring

10 sheets silver leaf

for the pistachio wafers

Butter, for greasing

3 egg whites

3½oz/95g caster sugar [½ cup superfine
  sugar]

3½oz/95g plain flour [⅔ cup all-purpose
  flour], sifted

2oz/50g [⅓ cup] unsalted pistachio nuts,
  unpeeled

You will also need 10 x 4floz/120ml plastic kulfi moulds or ramekins, a 1lb/450g loaf pan, baking parchment and 10 squares of banana leaf

Blend the pistachios for the kulfi in a food processor until they are very finely chopped but not yet an oily paste.

Add the rest of the ice-cream ingredients, except the silver leaf, and blend again, for 1 minute, until fairly smooth. Divide the mixture between the moulds, cover and freeze for 5 hours, or until frozen.

Grease the loaf pan lightly and line it with parchment paper. Heat the oven to 350°F/180°C/Gas 4.

Whisk the egg whites for the wafers with an electric mixer until stiff and gradually whisk in the sugar 1 tblsp at a time.

Fold the flour and nuts into the meringue to make a soft, sponge-like mixture. Spoon into the loaf pan and smooth the top over. Bake for 40 minutes until firm and golden.

Turn the loaf out on to a wire rack to cool and remove the paper. Reduce the oven temperature to 275°F/140°C/Gas 1.

Slice the cooled loaf as thinly as possible with a sharp, fine-bladed knife and lay the slices on baking trays.

Bake the wafers for 6 minutes, until barely coloured. Transfer them to a wire rack to cool and crisp up.

Dip the ice-cream moulds in very hot water for 5 seconds. Run a small knife around the edges and turn the kulfi onto plates lined with squares of banana leaf.

Lift the silver leaf off its paper with the tip of a knife and use it to decorate the kulfi. Serve with the pistachio wafers.

Advance preparation: make the wafers 1 week before and store in an airtight box layered with parchment paper.
Freezing: freeze the kulfi 1 week ahead.

Gilded sachertorte

The only chocolate cake I ever make is this one, which has good keeping qualities and freezes very well. I vary it by changing the decoration. Often, it's simply festooned with fresh flowers. Other decorating ideas follow this basic recipe. SERVES 20

for the chocolate sachertorte
3 large eggs, whole + 12 large eggs, separated
1lb2oz/500g caster sugar [2½ cups granulated sugar]
1lb6oz/625g dark, semi-sweet chocolate
12oz/350g [4 cups] ground almonds
1 tblsp freshly ground coffee grains
for the icing
1lb/450g dark, semi-sweet chocolate
6oz/175g [¾ cup] unsalted butter, cubed + extra for greasing
4 tblsp smooth apricot jam
for the gilded decoration
12 sheets 23.5-24 carat transfer gold leaf
12 cape gooseberries, papery skins peeled back
You will also need a 10in/25.5cm round cake pan, some parchment paper, newspaper and string

Line the base and insides of the greased pan with parchment paper. Wrap 4 layers of newspaper around the outside of the pan and tie with string. Heat the oven to 375°F/190°C/Gas 5.
Beat the whole eggs, egg yolks and sugar in an electric mixer for 10 minutes.
Melt the chocolate for the cake in a bowl over a pan of hot water. Stir it into the egg mixture with the almonds and coffee.
Whisk the egg whites until stiff and carefully fold into the egg mixture.
Pour the mixture into the cake pan and bake for 1½ hours. Cover the top of the cake with damp parchment paper and dampen it every 20 minutes while baking. The cake is cooked when a skewer inserted in the middle comes out clean.
Cool the cake in the cake pan for 1 hour before turning it out onto a wire rack.
Melt the chocolate for the icing in a bowl over a pan of hot water. Add the butter, bit by bit, stirring well. Cool the icing until it sets to a thick pouring consistency.

Trim the top of the cake, if necessary, and turn it upside down on the wire rack.
Melt the jam in a small pan over a low heat, then brush it over the cake.
Pour the icing over the cake and smooth it evenly over the top and sides. Let the icing set for 2 hours before decorating.
Lay a sheet of gold leaf with its backing paper still on in the centre of the cake. Use the back of a small round-bladed knife to gently rub the paper, transferring the gold onto the cake.
Remove the paper and continue to work your way around the cake with the rest of the gold leaf until the top is covered.
Arrange the cape gooseberries on top of the gilded cake and serve.

Advance preparation: bake the cake 1 week ahead, wrap well in 2 layers of foil and store in an airtight box in a cool place. Ice up to 2 days ahead and store uncovered in the fridge (the condensation will disappear 4 hours after taking it out). Decorate 8 hours before and keep cool.
Freezing: freeze the cake, wrapped as above, in an airtight box, 8 weeks before.

40-something cake

If piping messages onto cakes isn't your forte, use chocolate numbers or letters. SERVES 20

1 x Chocolate Sachertorte Recipe (left)
⅓ (5½oz/165g) x Chocolate Cookie Dough Recipe (page 84)
Flour, for rolling
2 tsp icing sugar [confectioners' sugar]
2 tsp unsweetened cocoa powder
You will also need the appropriate 2in/5cm number cutters

Make and ice the cake as above.
Roll the dough out on a lightly floured surface until ¼in/5mm thick. Stamp out 24 numbers using the cutters and transfer to baking trays. Chill for 30 minutes.
Heat the oven to 350°F/180°C/Gas 4 and bake the cookies for 8 minutes. Lift onto a wire rack to cool.
Make small incisions in the cake with a sharp knife and poke the biscuits in, at random, so that they stand up.

40-something cake

Dust the icing sugar and cocoa lightly over the top of the cake before serving.

Advance preparation: decorate the cake up to 2 hours in advance and keep cool.
Freezing: refer to basic recipe.

Heart cake with rosepetals

This wedding cake can double as the dessert if served with some fresh berries, or kissel (page 132). You can also use this recipe to make 30 individual heart-shaped cakes about 3in/7.5cm wide. SERVES 50-60

1½ x Chocolate Sachertorte Recipe (left)
10 large unsprayed roses, petals removed
You will also need a heart-shaped cake pan 12½in/31cm wide x 3½in/9cm deep

Make the cake as above but bake for 2-2½ hours at 375°F/190°C/Gas 5.
Decorate the iced cake by arranging the rose petals in a heart-shape on top.

Advance preparation: decorate 1-2 hours before serving and keep cool.
Freezing: refer to basic recipe.

Left: *use cinnamon sticks to stir steaming cups of Hot Buttered Rum – they add a festive element to the party and a delicious flavour to the drink. Below: easy-to-make Roast Beef Salad is a rustic blend of Mediterranean storecupboard ingredients with a piquant creamy horseradish dressing.*

festive

Clockwise from top right: *simple but stunning – Tomato Salad is made stylish with a variety of different shapes and colours, then dressed with balsamic vinaigrette, capers and marjoram leaves; a pretty dusting of fine sugar gives this Apricot Tart, made from fresh fruit, a seasonal look; the secret of any successful buffet menu is not only in choosing dishes that taste delicious, they must also maintain their attractive appearance throughout the party and have guests coming back for second helpings.*

the menu

Chicory with roquefort, pecans & cranberries

Roast beef salad

Jambalaya

Tomato salad

Borlotti & green beans

Apricot tart

Chocolate martini

Ginger cordial with star anise ice-cubes

Hot buttered rum

Left: *cubes of star anise set in ice make this ginger-flavoured cocktail special. It contains no alcohol, ensuring that all guests feel welcome and cared for.*
Below: *an example of good menu planning – two hearty dishes, one hot, one cold, with differing textures, colours and flavours. Guests can enjoy one, or both.*

Clockwise from above:
Borlotti & Green Beans can be served warm or cold; the classic martini is given a festive edge with a chocolate-rimmed glass and a curl of orange peel; traditional seasonal flavours of pecans, blue cheese and cranberries combined in a canapé; prawn Jambalaya is hearty food for cold evenings, and easy to eat with a fork.

drinks

Guests want to eat, yes, but they also want to **drink and be merry**. Anyone can open a few bottles. Hosts with the most know the value of frivolity. **Kick-start** your party with a fun and funky **cocktail** – with or without alcohol. A fabulous frappé, a mesmerising mojito, a martini glass **with chocolate stuck on it**. Fresh **fruits** are a focal point, whether embedded in ice-cubes or creamed into a cooler. There's a small collection of **classics**, such as **Whisky Sours** and Negronis, for people who know what they like and want to stick with it. But we also **add sparkle** to old favourites, scooping **sorbet** into champagne, blending gold leaf into vodka, secreting an oyster in Clamato **juice**. You can run **hot and cold** in this chapter, with spicy warmers for indoors and out, for supping by the bonfire, or bidding **farewell** to guests as they **venture** into the cold night air. And if you find anyone has not gone home, whip up the recipe for **Breakfast in a Glass**, remembering that **one mint julep** was not the cause of it all.

Sugar syrup

This recipe can be used for sweetening alcoholic and non-alcoholic drinks, or for adding to fruit sauces to serve with desserts. MAKES 1 PINT/ 570ML [2½CUPS]

15floz/425ml water
15oz/425g [2 cups + 2 tblsp] sugar

Put the water in a pan, bring to the boil, add the sugar and stir continuously for about 30 seconds until the sugar has dissolved. To prevent the syrup crystallizing, it is important that the sugar has completely dissolved before you reduce the heat to a low setting.
Simmer the syrup for 5 minutes. Remove it from the heat and cool before using, or storing in the fridge.

Advance preparation: make up to 3 weeks ahead, cover and chill.
Freezing: not suitable.

Fruited ice-cubes

Fruited ice-cubes look beautiful floating in summery drinks, or even in a glass of sparkling mineral water. Citrus peel, edible flower petals such as borage and rose petals, and fresh cranberries for Christmas or Thanksgiving drinks, can also be used instead of the soft fruit.

Lemons or cucumber
A selection of soft fruit such as
  blackberries, cherries, raspberries,
  redcurrants & strawberries
Water
You will also need several ice-cube trays

Remove the peel from the lemons, or cucumber, in a coil using a canelle knife [citrus stripper]. Tie the strips into knots.
Divide the fruits and the knotted peel between the ice-cube trays, top up with water and freeze for 4-6 hours.
Remove the ice-cubes from the trays and add to drinks just before serving.

Advance preparation: see below.
Freezing: make the ice-cubes up to 7 days in advance.

Lime, orange & lemon citrus pressé

If you want to decorate this refreshing drink with citrus peel knots, make them before you juice the fruit. Use a canelle knife [citrus stripper] to remove a coil of rind and then just twist this rind into a knot. MAKES 10

10floz/275ml lime juice
10floz/275ml orange juice
10floz/275ml lemon juice
10floz/275ml sugar syrup
1½ pints/850ml [3½ cups] sparkling
  mineral water
Ice-cubes, for serving

Mix all the ingredients together and serve poured over ice. Decorate with citrus peel knots, if desired.

Advance preparation: make the knots and mix the juices up to 6 hours before, cover and chill. Add the water to order.
Freezing: squeeze and freeze the juices up to 2 weeks ahead.

Ginger cordial with star anise ice-cubes

Refreshing and aromatic, this is a good thirst quencher on hot days and accompanies Asian foods extremely well. SERVES 10

20 star anise
8oz/225g stem ginger in syrup
4 pints/2.25 litres [10 cups] sparkling
  mineral water

Freeze the star anise with plain water in ice-cube trays for 4-6 hours.
Blend the stem ginger with all of its preserving syrup and a little of the mineral water in a food processor for about 1 minute or until really well puréed.
Divide the mixture between glasses, top up with the remaining water and stir well.
Add the star anise ice-cubes and serve.

Advance preparation: purée the ginger, cover and chill up to 7 days ahead. Dilute the ginger cordial to order.
Freezing: make the ice-cubes up to 7 days in advance.

Limey

This cooling summer drink can also be diluted with soda water instead of mineral water if you prefer. MAKES 10

10floz/275ml lime juice
10floz/275ml lemon juice
2 pints/1.2 litres [5 cups] sparkling
  mineral water
Angostura or other bitters, to taste
Ice-cubes, for serving

Mix the lime and lemon juice together.
Pour on the mineral water, stir and add
the bitters to taste. Serve over ice.

Advance preparation: mix the juices up
to 6 hours before, cover and chill. Add the
mineral water and bitters to order.
*Freezing: squeeze and freeze the lime
and lemon juices up to 2 weeks before.*

Jasmine infusion

*Scented edible flowers and herbs, such as
jasmine, borage, elderflower and variegated
applemint can be used to make this delicate
infusion. Use sugar-encrusted swizzle sticks
as decorative stirrers.* MAKES 10

A handful of unsprayed jasmine flowers
  + a few extra for decoration
2½ pints/1.5 litres [1½ quarts] boiling
  water
10 sugar swizzle sticks

Put the jasmine flowers into a large
cafetière and pour over the boiling water.
Leave them to infuse for 5 minutes
before plunging the pot.
Pour the infusion into glasses, add a
jasmine flower to each for decoration and
serve with the sugar swizzle sticks.

Advance preparation: not suitable.
Freezing: not suitable.

left Fruited ice-cubes

Clear gazpacho

Serve small glasses of this clear tomato water, studded with tiny diced gazpacho vegetables, to greet your guests on a hot day, or to start a meal. Use really ripe tomatoes for the best results. MAKES 10

for the tomato water
4lb/1.8kg beefsteak tomatoes (to yield about 2½ pints/1.5 litres [1½ quarts] tomato water), quartered
2 tblsp salt
for the gazpacho vegetable garnish
1 beefsteak tomato
½ cucumber, finely diced
½ small yellow sweet pepper
½ medium avocado
1 rounded tblsp finely snipped chives
Freshly ground black pepper
You will also need some large squares of muslin or cheesecloth

Line a large sieve or colander with 2 layers of muslin and place over a bowl.
Blend the tomatoes and salt together for the tomato water in a food processor until well chopped.
Pour the tomato pulp into the sieve, cover and leave for 8 hours in the fridge so that the liquid drips through into the bowl. Do not force the pulp.
Remove the tomato pulp and reserve it for another dish. Season the remaining liquid with pepper and salt if it needs it.
Put the tomato for the gazpacho vegetable garnish into a bowl, cover with boiling water and leave for 10 seconds. Plunge the tomato into cold water, then peel, quarter and discard the seeds.
Dice the flesh finely and mix it with the cucumber, pepper, avocado and chives.
Mix the vegetables and chives into the clear tomato water, divide between glasses and serve chilled.

Advance preparation: make the tomato water 2 days ahead; dice the cucumber and pepper 1 day before, cover and chill. Prepare the avocado and chives to order.
Freezing: not suitable.

right Clear gazpacho

Berry frappé

This deep burgundy-coloured frappé is a good way of using up any leftover soft berries that you have. Use the best that's in season, substituting blackberries, loganberries and strawberries if necessary. MAKES 10

1lb 14oz/850g mixed berries, such as
  blackcurrants, redcurrants & raspberries
1lb 14oz/850g [4 cups] ice-cubes
1½ pints/850ml [3½ cups] sugar syrup
10floz/275ml lime juice
2 pints/1.2 litres [5 cups] cold water

Put the berries on a tray lined with plastic wrap. Freeze uncovered for 1½-2 hours, or until the berries are frozen solid.
Divide the frozen berries and ice into 4 batches. Put the first batch into a food processor and pulse about 5 or 6 times until everything is evenly crushed.
Add a quarter of the sugar syrup, lime juice and water and blend briefly, just enough to combine everything.
Pour into a jug. Repeat with the remaining batches and serve immediately.

Advance preparation: not suitable.
Freezing: freeze the berries up to 4 weeks before and cover.

Strawberries & cream frappé

Crushed berries and cream over ice – of all the frappés, this is my favourite. MAKES 10

3lb/1.35kg strawberries, halved
1lb 14oz/850g [4 cups] ice-cubes
1½ pints/850ml sugar syrup
2 pints/1.2 litres single cream [5 cups
  light cream]

Put the strawberries on a tray lined with plastic wrap and freeze uncovered for 2 hours or until they are frozen solid.
Divide the frozen strawberries and ice into 4 batches and put the first batch in a food processor. Pulse about 5 or 6 times until evenly crushed.
Pour in a quarter of the sugar syrup and cream. Quickly blend for a few seconds just to incorporate the ingredients.

Pour the frappé mixture into a jug and repeat with the remaining batches. Serve immediately in glasses.

Advance preparation: not suitable.
Freezing: freeze the strawberries up to 4 weeks before and cover.

Watermelon frappé

Adding sugar syrup to this frappé enhances the watermelon's elusive taste. MAKES 10

1lb 14oz/850g [4 cups] ice-cubes
5lb/2.25kg [14 cups] watermelon flesh,
  seeded & cut into 1in/2.5cm chunks
1 pint/570ml [2½ cups] sugar syrup

Put a quarter of the ice-cubes into a food processor and pulse until crushed.

Add a quarter of the melon and the sugar syrup and pulse a further 2 or 3 times so that the melon is smooth but the ice retains a crushed texture.
Pour the mixture into a jug. Repeat with the remaining batches and serve immediately in glasses.

Advance preparation: cut the melon, cover and chill up to 4 hours ahead.
Freezing: not suitable.

Clockwise from top right Strawberries & cream frappé, Berry frappé & Watermelon frappé

Coconut cooler

As this coconut drink isn't overly sweet it's a good cooling accompaniment to hot, spicy Thai and Indian curries. Sometimes I use plain yogurt, instead of milk and cream, to make it into more of an Indian lassi-style drink. MAKES 10

2 pints/1.2 litres [5 cups] coconut milk
1½ pints/850ml [3½ cups] milk
10floz/275ml single cream [light cream]
10oz/275g [3½ cups] fresh coconut flesh,
  the brown skin removed
10floz/275ml sugar syrup
Ice-cubes, for serving
10 small pieces fresh coconut flesh,
  to decorate

Divide all of the ingredients into
4 batches, except for the ice and the
pieces of coconut for decorating.
Blend each batch in a food processor for
about 1 minute or until the mixture is
completely smooth.
Pour over ice into glasses and decorate
with the coconut flesh. Serve.

Advance preparation: make the cooler
up to 6 hours ahead, cover and chill.
Add ice to order.
*Freezing: make and freeze the cooler up
to 2 weeks before.*

Kiwi cooler

Packed with vitamins C and E, not only do kiwi fruit make healthy drinks, but their vivid colour speckled with fine black seeds makes them an attractive addition to any drinks tray. MAKES 10

2½lb/1.15kg kiwi fruit, peeled and
  quartered + an extra 10 quarters,
  unpeeled, to decorate
1½ pints/850ml [3½ cups] cold water
1 pint/570ml [2½ cups] sugar syrup
10floz/275ml lemon juice
Ice-cubes, for serving

Divide the peeled kiwi fruit, water, sugar
syrup and lemon juice into 4 batches and
then blend each batch in a food processor
for about 45 seconds or until smooth.

Pour over ice into glasses and decorate with the remaining kiwi fruit. Serve.

Advance preparation: make the cooler up to 6 hours ahead, cover and chill. Add ice to order.
Freezing: make and freeze the cooler up to 2 weeks before.

Mango & passionfruit cooler

Really ripe mangoes and passionfruit are essential for this particular cooler. Don't even think about making it unless they are both ripe. The best passionfruit are slightly wrinkled with an intensely flavoured, deep orange pulp, whilst the most succulent variety of mango has sunset colours of red and orange. If ripe mangoes are hard to come by, Indian and Asian shops also sell the excellent Alfonso variety in cans. MAKES 10

5 large mangoes (to yield
   2½ pints/1.5 litres [1½ quarts] purée)
10 passionfruit + an extra 5 passionfruit,
   halved, to decorate
1 pint/570ml [2½ cups] sugar syrup
1 pint/570ml [2½ cups] lime juice
Ice-cubes, for serving

Blend the mangoes in a food processor until smooth then pass through a sieve.
Remove the seeds and juice from 10 of the passionfruit and combine them in a jug with the mango purée, sugar syrup, and lime juice.
Pour the mixture over ice into glasses. Decorate each glass with a passionfruit half and serve.

Advance preparation: make the cooler up to 6 hours ahead, cover and chill. Add ice to order.
Freezing: make and freeze the cooler up to 2 weeks before.

*Left to right Kiwi cooler,
Mango & passionfruit cooler,
Coconut cooler*

Breakfast in a glass
Great for Sunday brunches, but also for days when breakfast is on the run. MAKES 10

2 pints/1.2 litres [5 cups] pink grapefruit,
   or ruby orange juice
2 pints/1.2 litres [5 cups] plain low-fat
   yogurt
10 tblsp clear honey
10 tblsp wheatgerm
Ice-cubes, for serving

Blend everything, except for the ice, together in a food processor. Pour over ice and serve.

Advance preparation: make up to 8 hours ahead, cover and chill.
Freezing: not suitable.

Spiced apple & cinnamon warmer
Serve this on wintry nights at the start of a party or just before everybody departs. Dark rum or calvados can be added. MAKES 10

4in/10cm piece root ginger, thinly sliced
4 star anise
12 cloves
2 cinnamon sticks
3½ pints/2 litres [2 quarts] unsweetened
   apple juice
4 tblsp clear honey
4 tblsp lemon juice
*You will also need a small piece of muslin
or cheesecloth and a piece of string*

Tie the ginger and spices in the muslin.
Place the spice bag and the rest of the ingredients in a medium-sized pan and heat gently for 30 minutes without boiling.
Remove from the heat and discard the spice bag. Pour the drink into glasses, placing a teaspoon in each to prevent cracking. Serve piping hot.

Advance preparation: make, cover and chill up to 1 week ahead. Reheat and pour into a hot thermos flask up to 2 hours before serving.
Freezing: make and freeze up to 2 weeks in advance.

Champagne & sorbet fizz

This is a grown-up version of an ice-cream soda. MAKES 10

10oz/275g sorbet, such as blackcurrant, melon, peach, raspberry, or strawberry
2 bottles champagne or other sparkling white wine
You will also need an ice-cream scoop

Make 10 small balls from the sorbet. Transfer to a tray, cover and freeze.
Chill the champagne glasses.
Place a scoop of sorbet in the bottom of each glass and slowly fill with champagne. Serve immediately.

Advance preparation: chill the glasses.
Freezing: scoop the sorbets and freeze up to 3 days before.

Poinsettia

A lovely champagne cocktail to serve at autumn drinks parties. MAKES 10

15floz/425ml cranberry juice
5floz/150ml Cointreau or Grand Marnier
2 bottles champagne or other sparkling white wine

Mix the cranberry juice and liqueur together and divide between glasses. Top with champagne and serve immediately.

Advance preparation: mix the juice and liqueur up to 4 hours before, cover and chill. Top up with champagne to order.
Freezing: not suitable.

Whisky sour

Fresh lemon juice is vital to give this drink its distinctive sour flavour. MAKES 10

1 pint/570ml [2½ cups] Scotch whisky
10floz/275ml lemon juice
5floz/150ml sugar syrup
3 egg whites

Divide the ingredients into batches. Pour each batch into a cocktail shaker and shake briefly. Pour into glasses and serve.

Advance preparation: squeeze the lemons 2 hours before, cover and chill.
Freezing: not suitable.

Mojito

This Cuban rum punch is a variation of the original daiquiri made famous by Ernest Hemingway. Top up with soda water for a longer, more refreshing drink. MAKES 10

1½ pints/850ml [3½ cups] light rum
10floz/275ml lime juice
5 tblsp sugar syrup
Ice-cubes, for serving
Wedges of lime, for decoration
Sprigs of mint, for decoration
Soda water, optional

Stir the rum, lime juice and sugar syrup together. Divide the ice between glasses, pour over the rum mixture, decorate with the lime wedges and mint and serve.

Advance preparation: mix the rum, lime juice and syrup up to 4 hours ahead, cover and chill. Pour over ice to order.
Freezing: not suitable.

Long Island iced tea

A misnomer if ever there was one – the colour of this drink is its only possible similarity to tea! Serve with lots of ice. MAKES 10

3½floz/100ml Bacardi
3½floz/100ml gin
3½floz/100ml vodka
3½floz/100ml tequila
3½floz/100ml Cointreau
7floz/200ml lime juice
3 pints/1.75 litres [7½ cups] Coca-Cola
Ice-cubes, for serving

Mix the spirits and the lime juice together, then divide between glasses half-filled with ice. Top up with Coke, stir and serve.

Advance preparation: mix the spirits and lime juice together up to 4 hours ahead, cover and chill. Top up with ice and cola to order.
Freezing: not suitable.

Morgan

Adding sloe gin to this cocktail gives it a deliciously intriguing flavour. MAKES 10

2½ pints/1.5 litres [1½ quarts] pink grapefuit juice
10floz/275ml sloe gin
10floz/275ml dry sherry
10floz/275ml Cointreau or Grand Marnier
3 tblsp crème de cassis
Ice-cubes, for serving

Mix all the ingredients together, pour over ice and serve.

Advance preparation: mix everything together, except the ice, up to 4 hours ahead, cover and chill. Add ice to order.
Freezing: not suitable.

Mint julep

It's essential to the success of this bourbon cocktail that you crush the mint leaves and sugar together to release the fragrance of the mint. MAKES 10

50 mint leaves
10 tsp caster sugar [granulated sugar]
3 tblsp water
1 pint/570ml [2½ cups] bourbon whiskey
Crushed ice, to serve
Sprigs of mint, for decoration

Put the mint, sugar and water together in a small jug. Crush the mint with the back of a spoon until the sugar has bruised the mint and dissolved.
Add the bourbon and mix well. Pour into glasses, top up with crushed ice and stir.
Decorate each glass with a sprig of mint and serve immediately.

Advance preparation: not suitable.
Freezing: not suitable.

right Mint julep

Oyster shooters

If you like oysters, then this is the drink for you! Serve well chilled in small glasses and knock them back in one. MAKES 10

10 small oysters
10floz/275ml Clamato juice, chilled
5floz/150ml ice-cold vodka
Freshly ground black pepper
½ small cucumber, finely diced

Put an oyster in the bottom of each glass.
Mix the Clamato juice, vodka, pepper and cucumber together and pour over the oysters. Serve immediately.

Advance preparation: dice the cucumber 1 day ahead, cover and chill. *Freezing: put the bottle of vodka in the freezer up to 8 hours before to chill.*

Chocolate martini

Purists won't approve of this martini. Not only have I added Cointreau, but it's also served in a chocolate-dipped glass. However, it's a fun party drink. A kumquat will substitute nicely for the twist of orange peel if you prefer. MAKES 10

2½oz/60g dark, semi-sweet chocolate,
    broken into squares
10floz/275ml ice-cold vodka or gin
15floz/425ml dry martini, chilled
5floz/150ml Cointreau, chilled
10 twists of orange peel, or 10 kumquats,
    to decorate

Melt the chocolate in a bowl over a pan of simmering water for 7-10 minutes or until melted.
Pour the chocolate onto a dinner plate, up-end the martini glasses and dip the rims into the chocolate. Gently shake to remove any excess, stand them upright and leave to harden.
Stir the vodka, dry martini and Cointreau together, pour into the chocolate-rimmed glasses and add the twist of orange peel or a kumquat. Serve icy cold.

left Simply red

Advance preparation: prepare the orange peel up to 2 hours before and put into plastic wrap.
Freezing: mix the vodka, dry martini and Cointreau together, cover and freeze up to 1 day ahead.

Simply red

This bright red cocktail of fruit juices with vodka, grenadine and bitters is equally delicious without any alcohol. MAKES 10

1 pint/570ml [2½ cups] cranberry juice
1 pint/570ml [2½ cups] blood orange juice or ruby orange juice
5 tsp grenadine
Angostura or other bitters, to taste
10floz/275ml vodka
Ice-cubes, for serving

Mix the juices together with the grenadine and bitters to taste. Add the vodka and pour over ice into glasses. Serve.

Advance preparation: mix all the ingredients together, except the ice, up to 4 hours before, cover and chill.
Freezing: not suitable.

Gold vodka

This is best drunk icy cold. Give the bottle a good shake before pouring so that the gold is held in suspension and serve the vodka with caviar-based canapés. Edible loose leaf gold is available from art shops. MAKES 10

1 pint/570ml [2½ cups] vodka
4 sheets 23.5 or 24 carat loose leaf gold

Pour the vodka into a blender. Lift the sheets of gold leaf off the backing paper with the tip of a knife and add to the vodka. Blend for 30 seconds.
Transfer the vodka back to the bottle and put in the freezer for 2 hours to chill.
Shake the bottle before serving and pour the vodka into small glasses.

Advance preparation: see below.
Freezing: freeze the gold vodka up to 4 weeks before.

Negroni

Count Camillo Negroni, a citizen of Florence in the 1920s, gave his name to this bitter Italian cocktail. MAKES 10

10floz/275ml Campari
10floz/275ml gin
10floz/275ml sweet vermouth
Ice-cubes, for serving

Mix all the ingredients together and pour over ice into glasses. Serve.

Advance preparation: mix up to 4 hours ahead, cover and chill. Pour over ice to order.
Freezing: not suitable.

Hot buttered rum

Let your guests add their own spiced butter to this warming drink and use cinnamon sticks instead of spoons to stir. MAKES 10

1 pint/570ml [2½ cups] dark rum
1 pint/570ml [2½ cups] boiling water
10 cinnamon sticks
for the spiced butter
2oz/50g [4 tblsp] unsalted butter, softened
2oz/50g [¼ cup] soft brown sugar
½ tsp ground cinnamon
½ tsp ground nutmeg
½ vanilla bean, split & the seeds scraped out, or ¼ tsp vanilla extract

Beat together all the ingredients for the spiced butter with a wooden spoon until creamy. Transfer to a serving bowl.
Heat the rum in a pan until very hot but not boiling, then add the boiling water.
Put a spoon in each glass to prevent them cracking, then pour in the rum mixture. Remove the spoons and add the cinnamon sticks.
Serve with the butter, allowing about 1 heaped teaspoon per glass. Stir well.

Advance preparation: mix the hot rum and boiling water together 2 hours before and put into a hot thermos flask.
Freezing: make the spiced butter up to 4 weeks ahead and freeze.

New Orleans coffee with chocolate spoons

Coffee spoons are dipped into melted chocolate for a frivolous touch. MAKES 10

for the spoons
2oz/50g plain, semi-sweet chocolate, broken into squares
for the New Orleans coffee
1 pint/570ml [2½ cups] strong hot coffee
1 tsp ground cinnamon
1 tblsp sugar
Pared zest of 2 oranges
Pared zest of 1 lemon
4floz/120ml brandy
4floz/120ml Cointreau or Grand Marnier
You will also need some muslin or cheesecloth and 10 coffee spoons

Melt the chocolate in a bowl over a pan of simmering water, for about 10 minutes.
Dip the spoons in the chocolate and put them on a plate. Chill for 45 minutes.
Remove the chocolate spoons from the fridge 10 minutes before serving.
Heat the coffee, cinnamon, sugar and both zests over a low heat in a pan. When hot, but not boiling, stir in the alcohol.
Strain the coffee through muslin and serve in cups with the chocolate spoons.

Advance preparation: dip the spoons up to 4 days ahead, cover and chill. Make the coffee up to 2 hours ahead, cool, then gently reheat for 10 minutes until hot.
Freezing: not suitable.

New Orleans coffee with chocolate spoons

Index

The first number given is the page on which the recipe appears.

Cook's notes

● Always follow one set of measurements – imperial or metric – throughout a recipe. American measures and terms are indicated by the use of square brackets [].

● Use cook's measuring spoons for accuracy:
1 teaspoon = 5ml;
1 tablespoon = 15ml.
All spoon measures are level unless otherwise stated.

● All vegetables are peeled unless otherwise stated.

● All eggs are large [extra large in the USA] unless otherwise stated.

● All garlic cloves are of a medium size unless otherwise stated.

● Where the word 'sugar' is used in isolation, British cooks should use white caster sugar and American cooks granulated sugar, however, slightly coarser grades can be used in these recipes if necessary. Where caster, confectioners', granulated, icing or superfine sugars are specified, it is imperative to the success of the recipe that the named variety is used.

● It may seem that in some of the advance preparation instructions it is not worth spending time preparing tiny amounts of food ahead of time. However, if you are making these recipes for large numbers, it is worthwhile.

● The elderly, children, pregnant women and those suffering from immune deficiency diseases should avoid eating raw or lightly cooked eggs due to the potential risk of salmonella.

● If you are unsure whether any of your guests are allergic to peanuts or peanut oil, always use olive oil or sunflower oil rather than oils labelled groundnut, peanut or vegetable for safety.

Acknowledgments

There are so many people involved in the production of a book and this one is no exception.

I would particularly like to thank Lindsey Greensted-Benech, our wonderful head cook at Lorna Wing Ltd for 14 years, who did all the testing and cooking of the recipes for this book and prepared the food for photography. She deserves accolades for her patience, skill and dedication.

Thank you to the team who helped produce the book: Jan Baldwin for her impeccable eye and stunning photography, Peter Dixon, Jan's able assistant, and Sue Parker, whose superb styling enhanced our food enormously. At Conran Octopus, thanks go to Jenni Muir, for her constant encouragement and patience in editing the text and recipes; Leslie Harrington for her skill and expertise in art-directing the book so beautifully; and Mary Staples, the art editor, for implementing the design.

Maryse Boxer at Chez Joseph was generous in lending some of her fabulous collection of tableware for photography. Thanks also to Sophie Grigson, for generously allowing me to use her mother's recipe, Paula Pryke for the use of her flat for shooting, and to my literary agents, Felicity Rubinstein and Sarah Lutyens.

Martine de Gues gave practical advice whilst my partner Brian McCombie put up with having no social life and lots of leftovers for months on end. Chris Wing, my sister, deserves special thanks as she kept our catering business going in my long absence and made sure that everything continued to run smoothly. Thanks also go to the others at the company – Maria Radcliffe, Jonathan Attwood, Sue Hargreaves and Ged Deutrom – who took good care of all our clients whilst I was away.

There have been many people over the years who have supported and inspired me and I would like to thank them too. Early on in my career, Lady Elizabeth Anson of Party Planners gave me many wonderful opportunities to cook for some fascinating clients. Both Jasper and his father, Terence Conran, had an enormous impact on my cooking education and taught me so much about good food. Delia Smith and Michael Wynn Jones gave me my first opportunity to write and without them I would not have felt able to undertake this book.

Finally, there was my mother, Lottie, who encouraged me in the kitchen from a very early age and my father, Richard, who uncomplainingly ate all the dreadful, childish results. Thank you.